Preventing Litigation

Preventing Litigation

An Early Warning System *to Get* *Big Value out of Big Data*

Nelson E. Brestoff and William H. Inmon

BUSINESS EXPERT PRESS

Preventing Litigation: An Early Warning System to Get Big Value out of Big Data

Copyright © Business Expert Press, LLC, 2015.

First published in 2015 by
Business Expert Press, LLC
222 East 46th Street, New York, NY 10017
www.businessexpertpress.com

ISBN-13: 978-1-63157-315-6 (paperback)
ISBN-13: 978-1-63157-316-3 (e-book)

Business Expert Press Business Law Collection

Collection ISSN: 2333-6722 (print)
Collection ISSN: 2333-6730 (electronic)

Cover and interior design by Exeter Premedia Services Private Ltd., Chennai, India

First edition: 2015

10 9 8 7 6 5 4 3 2 1

Printed in the United States of America.

Nick Brestoff dedicates this book to Lois Montague Brestoff, his partner for life since 1975; to their sons Daniel R. Brestoff and Jonathan R. Brestoff Parker; and to his brother, Richard A. Brestoff.

Bill Inmon dedicates this book to his long-term counsel, Jim Bull, a lawyer and a friend.

Abstract

The legal profession must change. Today, attorneys don't think of ways to do less litigation. When the damage is done, they examine the wreck at the *bottom* of the cliff and offer to represent one side or the other.

Preventing Litigation, for the first time, explains how to build an *early warning system* to identify the risk of litigation before the damage is done, and proves that there is big value in less litigation.

This book puts everyone where they should be: at the *top* of the cliff.

The authors are subject matter experts, one in litigation, the other in computer science, and each coauthor has more than four decades of training and experience in their respective fields.

Together, they present a way forward to a transformative revolution for the slow-moving world of law for the benefit of the fast-paced environment of the business world.

Keywords

avoiding, reducing, preventing, managing, risk, litigation, Big Data, business intelligence, early warning system, in-house counsel, Legal Department, less litigation, potential litigation, preventive law

Contents

Foreword

My father, Louis M. Brown, was more importantly the father of Preventive Law. He wrote extensively on Preventive Law, from his first books, *Preventive Law* and *How to Negotiate a Successful Contract* to his last, *Lawyering Through Life*. He invented, proselytized, taught, and breathed Preventive Law. He wrote for law reviews, bar journals, newspapers, and even airline magazines. He taught Preventive Law at the University of Southern California Gould School of Law (USC) for over 20 years, but he also lectured whenever he could, at law schools around the country, in colleges, high schools, and at the dinner table.

Being a prophet is a lonely life. There were few disciples and a lot of doubters. The view that a lawyer's job is to keep clients out of court was in his day counterintuitive. Law school taught cases, not lawyering. Clinical education was just a toddler. He started the first university paralegal education program at USC. He installed law office classrooms in law schools so students could see lawyers at work and practice their skills in offices, not in a courtroom. He started the mock law office competition with just two schools because he convinced another professor to give it a go. Clinical programs are now endemic. The Mock Law Office Competition has since been renamed the Client Counseling Competition, and has been taken over by the American Bar Association (ABA) domestically and is in practically every ABA accredited law school. The Brown Mosten International Client Consultation Competition (www.brownmosten.com) this year had competitors from over 20 countries and is affiliated with the International Bar Association.

Dad was always searching for proof of concept, and data, to support his approach. When he saw a casebook full of cases, he went to the lawyer's office to find the files. What went wrong? When? He saw lawsuits and conducted legal audits and legal autopsies to find out what went wrong. But too often confidentiality and reticence blocked his path. There were few teaching materials and almost no data to demonstrate that lawyers could prevent litigation, and that prevention was worthwhile. He worked up audit manuals for corporate lawyers, tried to convince insurance companies to write policies, and promoted legal health and personal legal wellness check-ups.

He would be a lot less lonely now, and a proud grandfather of this book. Finally there is a scientific approach and data to support the theories and to help fashion smart approaches. He smiles. He told us so.

Harold A. Brown
Los Angeles, California
May 1, 2015

Acknowledgments

For reading one or more drafts of portions of this book and for their helpful comments, we thank Bing Baksh (CEO, Vita-Herb Nutriceuticals Inc.); Adolph Barclift (USEReady); Philip Beaver, PhD (Department of Business Information and Analytics, Daniels College of Business, University of Denver); Michael G. Becker (Computer Programming Consultant); Curt Brennan (Senior VP, UBCsoft); Joseph Busch, MLS (Taxonomy Strategies); Michael Cobb (Michael Cobb and Associates); Paul Davis (Senior Business Development Manager, CONNX Solutions); Ron Friedmann (Fireman & Company); Matthew Gertler (JD-MBA candidate; founder and president of the Entrepreneur and Venture Capital Association at the USC Gould School of Law); Harpal Gill (Senior VP, CONNX Solutions); Ron Gruner (CEO [ret.], Sky Analytics); Patty Haines, MS; Gary L. Henriksen, MD; Bonny Herman (President [ret.], Valley Industry & Commerce Assn.); Lynn Frances Jae (e-Discovery Writer); John Kelly (Business Development-Concurrent Technologies); Mark Leher, MBA (COO, WAND Inc.); Jonathan R. Brestoff Parker, PhD; Amar D. Sarwal, JD (VP and Chief Legal Strategist, Association of Corporate Counsel); and Will Thomsen, MBA, ASA, CFA.

Special thanks are due to Sean Doherty (former Technology Editor, Legaltech News) and to Norman Thomas, MBA, CPA (Senior VP Corporate Development, Litera) for extensive comments, editing, and suggestions; Ralph Gutierrez (PACER) for assistance with federal court caseload research; and Kathryn Holt (National Center for State Courts) for assistance with state court caseload research; and to Bonnie Roos, Librarian, and Jan Jacobson, Library Assistant, of the Jamestown S'Klallam Tribal Library in Blyn, WA, for providing a quiet and wonderful place to work.

All affiliations are for reference only, with no endorsement implied.

If we have forgotten anyone, we apologize. We are responsible for any remaining errors of any kind.

PART I

Introduction

CHAPTER 1

How to Solve a Mystery

Malcom Gladwell, author of *The Tipping Point, Blink, Outliers* and *David and Goliath*, has described decision making in the information age as if we have shifted from solving puzzles to solving mysteries. A puzzle, he suggests, is solvable by obtaining missing information, while a mystery is solvable by making sense of a problem awash in information.

In this sense, Gladwell *belled the cat*. We *are* awash in information, and the trick will be whether and how well we get value out of it.

Let's put this challenge in context. Barclay T. Blair is the founder and executive director of the Information Governance Initiative,[1] and he has put this sentiment in the Big Data context. In an October 2014 interview at an industry conference, Blair said, "I think the biggest Big Data risk is not being able to extract insight and value from your data. If an organization doesn't create that capability, they are falling behind because their competitors are doing it."[2]

Now let's narrow the risk to the topic we address. In this book, we have tried to answer the Big Data and information governance challenges in a particular way, by figuring out the average cost of *litigation*, and the value of avoiding it, by presenting a methodology to find the seeds of a potential lawsuit *before* the damage is done.

By bringing technology to bear on this challenge, we are trying to turn a page. In the future, we believe, lawyers will be able to identify litigation risks and enable their companies to take evasive action.

Now let's step back and set the stage. We begin with the first word in Big Data: Big. Just because the data is Big does not mean that we cannot obtain content and then understand that content *in context*. The problem of Big Data can be made tractable by creating tools to review tens of thousands of documents (or e-mails) and parse out the small portions of interest.[3]

In other words, we don't want to have to read 60,000 e-mails to understand that we might be looking at a particular risk. We want a computer to read 600,000 e-mails, find a risk of a particular type of lawsuit in some of them, and then present those particular e-mails to an attorney for review, analysis, and, best of all, action.

In this book, broadly speaking, the general field is risk. The specific field is the risk of litigation. We start with this question: why do we care? What's the value of avoiding a particular risk, the risk of litigation? What amount of costs can we avoid?

Then, to address this cost, since we start with too much information, we need some proficiency with computer science.

Who will be the users of these new tools to avoid risk? We think the answer is lawyers, and more particularly, in-house counsel, who will work side-by-side with IT personnel.

But the practice of law, these days, is itself divisible into two spheres, transactions and litigation. We will tackle litigation.

The second word in Big Data is Data. Data is, for humans, divisible into many spheres: graphics, numbers, special characters like punctuation marks, and words. We will be dealing primarily with words, but with the further understanding that we are dealing with the interface between human language and computer processing. In that world, we must appreciate that our words, when we type them, are digitized into ones and zeros.

Here again, we find two spheres: words in fields, referred to as structured data, and words that may be in a field, but which are otherwise input free-form, and which we call *un*structured data.

The classic example is an e-mail. In an e-mail, the structured data consists of metadata and the data (information) in fields: the *to, from, cc and bcc, date,* and *subject* fields. In the *subject* field, although risky material could be written there, we generally know to expect a topic. So in general we would only look for potential anomalies, such as the phrase *attorney-client* or the word *privileged* without naming an in-house attorney in the *to* or *from* fields, or where the sender sends a *bcc* back to himself or herself.

Then there is the *message* field. What we write there is entirely and deeply *un*structured.

We won't be leaving structured data entirely to the side, but our focus will be how to obtain meaning from the *unstructured* textual information. Because the English language is complicated and humans don't speak *digital*, the problem of getting meaning out of unstructured text is a difficult one. In fact, unstructured data is sometimes called *dark data*.

Yet getting meaning out of unstructured text, as it may pertain to *potential* litigation, is what we must do.

But because we know that economics will drive the business intelligence advances we explain here, we will start with the *pain*. By pain, we mean the costs that are currently draining money away from net profits and the consequent *value* of being able to see, in an enterprise's own data, the words and phrases that present a risk the enterprise will want to avoid. The words and phrases we want to see are more like the kindling we use to start a fire. We want an *early warning* that the kindling is being put into place. And we want to see that kindling as soon as possible, so that the company may be proactive and, hopefully, put the fire out.

Litigating attorneys already know, of course, that when a lawsuit arises, they will be awash in information. One problem has been that lawyers are typically not data centric. They struggle with the tools and methods in what used to be called discovery, and which is now eDiscovery. As we contend here, in-house counsel will be the first *data lawyers*, and we suggest here that they have mysteries to solve, which they don't even currently appreciate.

But that will change. It must.[4]

The profession will change, with in-house counsel leading the way, for two reasons: first, because they are responsible for reducing the cost of litigation, and, second, because they are closest to the data. In fact, they will always be closest to the data, now and in the future. They will still have to review and pay the bills from outside counsel and the eDiscovery vendors for handling the lawsuits they must oversee and manage when litigation happens. This is the present. But getting close to the *spend* is not where the enterprise wants its lawyers to be. When in-house counsel can tap into the internal communications and the documents generated by company employees to find the threats, then they will be close to the *risk*. This is the future.

We appreciate that business executives are upset with the cost of litigation. That *is* the pain. But they think the cost of litigation, when it happens, is a *given*. They budget for it and tolerate the overruns.

To get the attention of our business leaders, computer scientists, and attorneys, we too will *bell the cat* by calculating the average cost of a commercial tort lawsuit. In this way, we will start off by demonstrating that *preventing* a lawsuit has value.

Big Value.

CHAPTER 2

Orientation

Enterprise Legal Management

The context for the change we foresee is not the Internet. Instead, we predict it will take place *within* the enterprise; that is, the intranet. That's where the data of interest is initially created. That's the data we want attorneys to be able to see.

Of course, the in-house attorneys, led by a General Counsel or a Chief Legal Officer, already see the bills their employers pay, and they probably know the pain and the average cost of their company's caseload.

Such pain has become evident to the profession. The Association of Corporate Counsel (ACC) certainly sees it. The ACC is the professional association of enterprise counsel, so the news has come to them from far and wide. In fact, the ACC consists of 35,000 members employed by 10,000 organizations all over the world.[1] Having listened to so many voices, one of the goals of the ACC is to reduce the *spend* by in-house legal departments by *at least* 25 percent.[2] Yet another goal is to have *fewer disputes.*[3]

There are some tools for measuring and increasing efficiency. In general, however, these are management tools, and the industry has been grouped under the heading *Enterprise Legal Management* (ELM).

Gartner, Inc. (NYSE: IT) (Gartner) first recognized ELM when it identified eight vendors in its inaugural Magic Quadrant for ELM in 2013.[4] To be admitted into the ELM space, a vendor had to address four out of five capabilities. They are:

- Matter management—considered by Gartner to be at the *core of an ELM application platform*, due to this category dealing with all relevant data that is related to legal matters;

- Legal document management—according to Gartner, provides corporate counsel with the capabilities to manage the creation, revision, approval, and consumption of documents, paper and electronic;
- Financial or spending management—applicable to the tools an organization uses to create budgets and monitor spending;
- E-billing—Gartner describes this as programs that help third parties, meaning external law firms and other vendors, to deliver legal bills securely for review and payment; and
- Business process management—including workflows and automated processes.[5]

Notice, however, that there are no tools for attorneys to track internal communications, as in e-mails, text messages, or other forms of unstructured data. The reason for this is that, currently, there are no tools for in-house counsel to manage litigation *risks* while those risks are still behind the firewall.

But as litigators know, e-mails reveal intentions. So we will want to find those risky e-mails and other communications long before they turn into litigation catastrophes.

In this book, we open the door to electronic *preventive law* analytics. In doing so, we will take you on a journey, which, we hasten to say, is a more organized journey than the one we took. We will begin with how an experienced litigator (Brestoff) met a computer scientist (Inmon). Next we will describe the pain and *quantify* it. This part of our research provided us with more than a handful of business-relevant metrics.

Thus, this first section is more about business intelligence, and we think it's a good example of how to approach a problem that is awash in data. We were curious. We explored. As we will explain, we used our results to not only inform ourselves, but to find new information and insights that market analysts may find relevant.

As a preview, because the business information for the Fortune 500 was publicly available, we combined our initial findings with other data. As a result we were able to (audaciously) rerank the Fortune 100 into something new: the Litigation 100. We created the Litigation 100 by reranking the first 100 companies in the Fortune 500 not by revenue, as *Fortune* does, but by caseload.

Then, having derived an average litigation cost per case, we realized that we could calculate the litigation cost (in federal court, at least) of any particular company for any particular year. And since we could do that for any particular year, we could do it for any string of years, in order to see trends.

In addition, we taught ourselves how to calculate an enterprise *litigation cost as a percentage of profits or losses.* And then, using one of the Fortune 500's filters, we could even see which companies in a specific industry sector had a competitive advantage. If a company had to deal with less litigation, it had advantages: lower costs, for example, and less hassle.

As we went further, we began to see how to implement a solution to the problem. The solution was a litigation *early warning system.*

We believe that our overall result will reinvigorate the concept of *preventive law* for the legal profession. And that will be quite a change for a profession that changes so slowly. When this change occurs, we believe it will amount to a paradigm shift and a breakthrough for the legal profession in the digital age.

A Meeting of Different Minds

As you know now, we started with a *preventive law* idea that the world would be better off if there were a way to spot the *potential* for litigation and then act to prevent it. It turns out that this idea and a tool to implement it were being developed by the authors, two people with very different experiences and skill sets.

So when we met, we understood right away that we had a common goal. We wanted to show that there is at least one way to achieve a presently unappreciated holy grail of modern times: *less* litigation.

Bill Inmon's software is called Textual Extract, Transform, and Load (ETL). As software intended to glean *context* and meaning from unstructured text—such as e-mails, instant messages, and other forms of free-form textual communication—Textual ETL was fundamentally different from other approaches to business intelligence. These other approaches were focused on gathering up structured data and using software to see patterns in that data. Bill had seen the need for a way to make sense of unstructured text, and when he combined his programming skills with his mastery of relational databases, he accessed a key ingredient for success—speed.

To Bill, in 2010, the process looked like the overview in Figure 2.1.

One takeaway from Figure 2.1 is that there are *two* inputs to Bill's Textual ETL software: taxonomies *and* unstructured text. We'll explain both of these inputs, but we want to note, right from the start, that by using the term *taxonomies* we don't mean to exclude similar terms like controlled vocabularies and word clusters. The taxonomies are input to *configure* Textual ETL, while the unstructured text is input to be read *by* Textual ETL. So taxonomies are a way for Textual ETL to *operate on* unstructured text in order to be able to report out actionable business intelligence to a user.

Taxonomies? What are they? They are *not* the sort of hierarchical taxonomies you may remember from a biology class, where the flora and fauna are categorized from the general to the specific. We'll leave it there for now. Although we'll give examples later in the book, we are referring

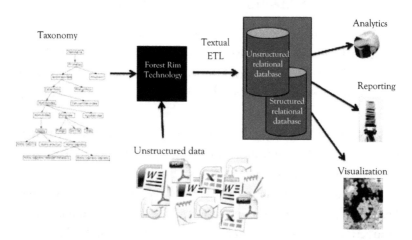

Figure 2.1 Bill Inmon's Overview circa 2010

to associative taxonomies, where a collection or cluster of words all generally describe or relate to a particular topic.

Bill began writing the code for Textual ETL somewhere around 2002 or 2003, and is still refining it. In 2010, Patty Haines, a computer scientist in her own right and one of Bill's colleagues, spent two weeks with a trucking company. The trucking company wanted to better understand the root cause of delayed shipments.

For the trucking company, shipments that were showing up late were troubling. In this scenario, data point A was a specific late shipment, a *service failure*. Data point B consisted of the in-the-field e-mails that were exchanged between the driver and dispatch. Data point C was the report the driver filed after making the delivery. Using Textual ETL circa 2010, could Patty connect the dots? Yes. She developed a dashboard (below) that showed not only the *service failure*, which, according to the driver's report, was *shipper-related*, but also the e-mails (the unstructured text) pertaining to that same incident, which indicated that, at the time, the driver reported a *computer failure*. This dashboard, shown in Figure 2.2, helped the company better understand the reason the shipment was late. If the delay was shipper-related, it was *not* the company's fault; but if there had been a computer failure, perhaps it was.

Now, quite a few of our early readers have commented to us that we are revealing too much information. We don't agree. We are using

Figure 2.2 Service failure dashboard

software to open up a new perspective on the field of law, and we can't expect anyone to walk along with us if we don't say enough about it.

Let's take another step back. Our personal histories might help explain *our* perspectives.

After an education in mathematics at Yale and computer science at New Mexico State University, W.H. (Bill) Inmon saw the growing use of computers to store data, and he became well-known as the father of the data warehouse. In fact, he coined the term. He organized the first conference. He's the author of over 50 books on data warehousing, and he's formed a company or two along the way.

So it stands to reason that he would know something about what a data warehouse would contain, as well as a topic we've already mentioned: Big Data.

Then, over a decade ago, Bill took on another challenge: wrestling with *unstructured* textual information. Over time, he wrote the code for Textual ETL.

Textual ETL addresses itself to textual information, not only the unstructured message portions of e-mails. Think text messages, tweets, transcribed voice mails, call center records, warranty claims, and so on.

Big Text.

Nick Brestoff's path was different. At the University of California at Los Angeles (UCLA), Nick was the science editor of the *Daily Bruin*, organized UCLA's first Earth Day, and earned a degree in systems engineering. He received a master's degree in Environmental Engineering Science from the California Institute of Technology, but then he turned to law. He stayed in the Los Angeles area and attended law school at the University of Southern California, which is where he met Law Professor Louis M. Brown (the subject of the Foreword), and was a member of the *Law Review*.

Briefly, from 1975 to early 2014, Nick started out as a prosecutor for the City of Los Angeles, and practiced law as a litigator in California. His clients were on both sides of the *v*, meaning that he represented both plaintiffs and defendants. For a few years in the 1990s, he was also a name partner in a law firm that specialized in coverage opinions and litigation monitoring services for insurance companies.

In 2006, the federal judiciary adopted new rules for the discovery of electronically stored information (ESI). Nick saw that information science and technology was roaring into the middle of every lawsuit. And he missed his educational roots in science and technology.

In 2010 and 2011, Nick also noticed that most lawyers were not prepared then (or now) to deal with this invasion of technology into their learned sphere. By then, Nick had become an eDiscovery expert, and had begun to write articles and teach online courses on the subject.[6]

Then, in 2011, while he was working on an eDiscovery project in connection with the Toyota unintended acceleration case, Nick remembered the teachings of Professor Brown. Professor Brown had been the father of *preventive law*. Wasn't there a way for Toyota to have seen this coming?

Professor Brown could not have asked this question. He had passed away in 1996 and never saw the computer revolution as it was unfolding. Back then, Windows 95 had just come out and Apple was nearly bankrupt. Steve Jobs didn't come back to Apple until December of 1996.

So in 2011, the phrase *preventive law* was stale. It was sometimes used for marketing purposes and, on occasion, a small number of legal academics wrote law review articles that focused on the topic. But there were *no* preventive law journals and no conferences.

One day in 2011, Nick took a lunch break to attend a seminar in the South Bay area of Los Angeles. The seminar was sponsored by The Data Warehouse Institute, and Bill Inmon was the speaker.

During his talk, Bill mentioned taxonomies and a company that specialized in them: WAND Inc.[7] During his talk, Bill also mentioned Textual ETL and said he was open to collaborating with anyone who had a good idea. During a break, Nick walked up to Bill and said he was thinking about a project and might want to speak with him about it one day.

In June 2012, after thinking about Professor Brown a lot and how to best apply his approach to litigation in our electronic age, Nick wrote and filed a provisional patent application for a project he called by various names: Project Searchlight was one; SWELL was another, but it was a backward acronym. It stood for the first letters of a *Litigation Liability Early Warning System*.[8]

Nick liked SWELL because the name reminded him of waves *before* they crested. Looking over and beyond the cresting waves was a way of seeing what was about to happen next. A litigation early warning system would be like that, he thought. He discarded the name because it was too much of an inside joke.

He finally settled on Intraspexion, a combination of a company's *intranet,* as in the computer infrastructure behind the firewall, and *introspection,* which is what the Greek philosophers were suggesting with the phrase Gnothi Sauton or *know thyself.*[9] To avoid litigation, Nick thought, corporations needed to think *inside* their own box, to be introspective.

On October 25, 2012, Nick planted his flag. He wrote an article entitled *Data Lawyers and Preventive Law,* and explained his vision of electronic *preventive law* analytics.[10] He was thinking that the time had come for preventive law to make a comeback. Only a handful of others have had a similar vision.[11]

But certainly, in the context of litigation, Big Data has arrived. So now instead of producing documents by giving opposing counsel a list of warehouses where boxes filled with paper documents could be found, a party was producing documents electronically and the volume was measured differently. The media were smaller, but the volume of documents was much larger, and could run into the terabyte range and higher.

Unfortunately, some silliness followed. Even though attorneys were not familiar with trying to examine so many documents to be produced electronically, the attorneys for the producing parties wanted to put their eyes on each piece of paper. So the documents that were produced electronically were printed out, to again become boxes filled with paper. That was the Gold Standard. The view was that only attorneys could discern which documents were not relevant and need not be produced, which documents were potentially relevant and must be produced, and which documents were relevant but must *not* be produced because they were privileged from being produced as either attorney work-product or because they were attorney-client communications.

But the volume of documents was enormous and soon the job was enormously boring as well as expensive. So the job of *tagging* the documents into these categories was outsourced to English-speaking lawyers in other countries.

On the other hand, many attorneys on the receiving end of the documents were equally silly. They didn't know what to do with the CDs they received. So they either didn't look at the CDs they received, which would have required them to know how to search the documents electronically, or they ordered them all to be printed out, and then they were back in the warehouse swamp.

The next major advance was to learn how to search ESI for the potentially relevant documents that had to be produced and how to find the few documents that would be persuasive to a jury: the smoking guns. Initially, the search technologies moved from simple searches using key words with Boolean connectors (such as *and, or,* and *not*) to negotiations over complex searches using hundreds of key words.[12] The next major advances involved either reducing the amount of data to review or using computer-assisted technologies, which we will discuss in a later chapter.

Then Nick remembered that Bill Inmon had mentioned WAND and taxonomies. He made a cold call to WAND, dropped Bill's name, and asked for a meeting. He met with WAND's founder, Ross Leher, and Ross's son, Mark, WAND's Chief Operating Officer; then with Bill Inmon.

It was late January 2013. Bill explained Textual ETL while Nick talked up electronic *preventive law* and how it could apply to litigation.

As a result, Nick agreed to form a Board of Advisors. He soon located Law Professor Thomas D. Barton at the California Western School of Law in San Diego. He is the Louis and Hermione Brown Professor of Law and Director of the Louis M. Brown Program in Preventive Law. He is also the Coordinator of the National Center for Preventive Law.

Professor Barton agreed to join the Board of Advisors and referred Nick to Professor Brown's son, Harold A. Brown, a partner in one of the preeminent entertainment law firms in Los Angeles, Gang, Tyre, Ramer & Brown.

Professor Barton had also written a book in 2009 about preventive law.[13] He sent Nick a copy. One of the chapter authors was James P. Groton. Jim Groton is a retired partner of the Atlanta powerhouse law firm of Sutherland Asbill & Brennan. Groton had used preventive law in the construction industry for years, implementing proactive techniques for encouraging cooperative behavior, defusing and de-escalating disagreements, and making sure that whenever unexpected events occurred the parties focused first on *fixing the problem* rather than *fixing the blame*. His favorite technique was to have a *standing neutral* available to periodically visit the jobsite of major projects. His approach was that the sooner an objective *neutral* could hear about and address a disagreement between the parties on the project, the better. He proved that the mere availability of a standing neutral usually encouraged the parties to resolve any problems between them without even having to ask the neutral to address them: a true preventive device.

Groton had become famous for his innovative work in preventing construction disputes. In retirement, he has expanded his prevention work to *keeping the peace* in other business contexts, including oil and gas industry relationships.

Groton is also a longtime member of the Panel of Distinguished Neutrals of the International Institute for Conflict Prevention and Resolution. On his website, he quotes Abraham Lincoln who, in 1840, said:

> Discourage litigation, persuade your neighbors to compromise whenever you can. Point out to them how the nominal winner is often a real loser—in fees, expenses, and waste of time. As a peacemaker the lawyer has a superior opportunity of being a good man. There will still be business enough.[14]

Groton agreed to Nick's request to join the Board. He believes in advancing the cause of preventive law whenever he can.

Eventually, Nick also found a few scholarly preventive law articles, the sort that appeared in law review journals. One article was written by Z. Jill Barclift, a law professor at the Hamline University School of Law in St. Paul, Minnesota.[15] Professor Barclift was also the Director of the Business Law Institute at Hamline. She said yes.

Nick was three for three. Now, with confidence, he approached Professor Brown's son, Harold. He had written a law review article with his father.[16] He said yes. That yes was a major boost. Would-be entrepreneurs with an idea need encouragement.

PART II

Proof of Value

CHAPTER 3

How Litigious Are We?

So to this point, what have we done? To litigators and writers both, we've not done too much more than a little throat-clearing. Having worked our way past the preliminaries, let's wade into the data. Is it true that, given the undeniable explosion of data, there is an explosion of *litigation* as well? How much litigation is there?

Anecdotally, we had heard the gripe that there was too much litigation. But we are driven by data and we wanted to answer this question. At least initially, we looked at the data in the federal court system. We offer it not only to help make a point but to introduce you to the federal court system itself and to how we learned to navigate it.

First, the data we report originates only from the federal court system called PACER. PACER is an acronym for Public Access to Court Electronic Records. All of the lawsuits initially filed in any of the federal district (trial) courts anywhere in the country can be accessed via PACER.[1]

Attorneys don't use PACER the way we use it here. Attorneys (and the courts) build document *towers* for each case as they prosecute, defend, and oversee it. The tower usually begins when a plaintiff files a Complaint. The Complaint is usually the first document filed. PACER gives it the creative name of Document 1.[2] From there, the document tower rises up.

Figure 3.1 shows a screenshot of what a document tower looks like when PACER is instructed to show the earliest date first.

As you can see in the figure, the tower starts with Document No. 1, the Complaint. After that, PACER gives a number to the next document, and the next, and so on, along with their respective dates and descriptions.

The federal courts are, of course, located all around the various states, and so PACER is a nationwide system. Cases are filed in PACER whenever they come in. They come in randomly from wherever they originate. PACER assigns a number to the case when it is filed, such as 4:14-cv-00095-SBA in the first line below the dark menu bar in

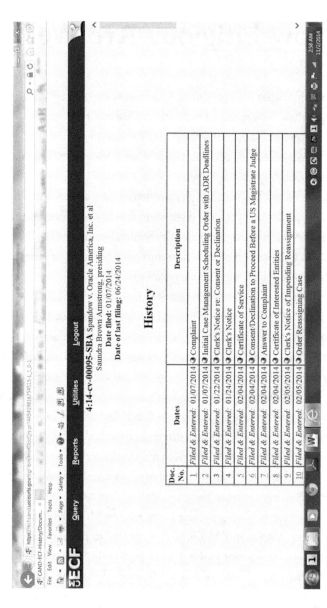

Figure 3.1 PACER's case history (sorted by oldest date first)

Figure 3.1, and a federal district court judge is randomly assigned (from each regional district court's panel of judges) to the case.[3]

In Figure 3.2, we present a Civil Cover Sheet. The Civil Cover Sheet is ancillary to the Complaint, so PACER does not list it as a case document. The Civil Cover Sheet is given a number to relate it to the Complaint, Document 1, such as 1-1. Attorneys typically regard the Civil Cover Sheet as being merely a form that the *system* requires. They pay no attention to it after signing it. The Civil Cover Sheet is a one-page form that lists a host

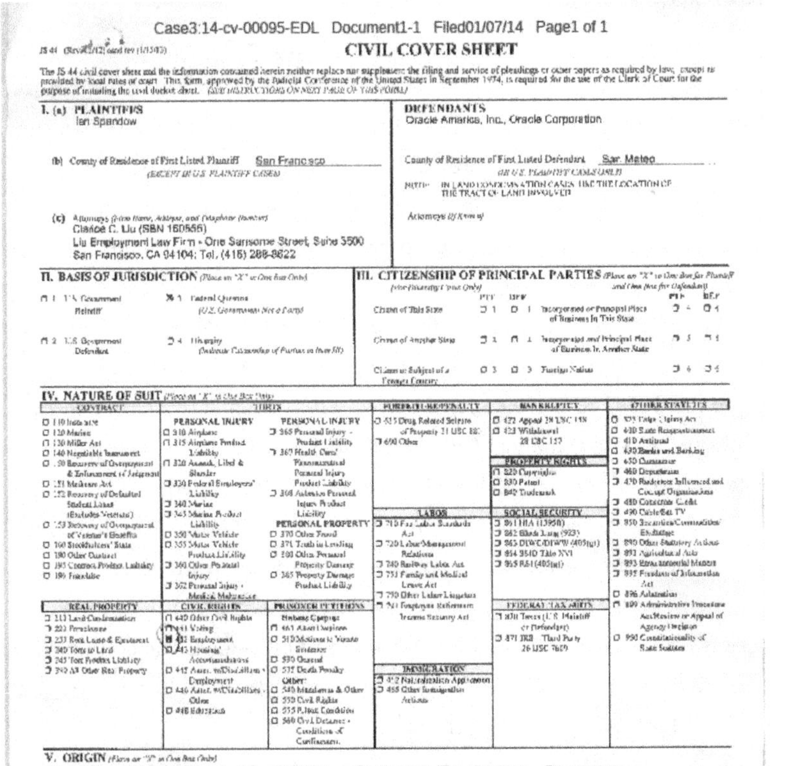
Case3:14-cv-00095-EDL Document1-1 Filed01/07/14 Page1 of 1

CIVIL COVER SHEET

I. (a) PLAINTIFFS: Ian Spandow

DEFENDANTS: Oracle America, Inc., Oracle Corporation

(b) County of Residence of First Listed Plaintiff: San Francisco

County of Residence of First Listed Defendant: San Mateo

(c) Attorneys: Clarice C. Liu (SBN 160556), Liu Employment Law Firm - One Sansome Street, Suite 3500, San Francisco, CA 94104; Tel. (415) 288-8622

II. BASIS OF JURISDICTION

III. CITIZENSHIP OF PRINCIPAL PARTIES

IV. NATURE OF SUIT

V. ORIGIN

VI. CAUSE OF ACTION: 42 U.S.C. Section 2000e et seq. — Title VII - Employment Discrimination And Retaliation

VII. REQUESTED IN COMPLAINT: JURY DEMAND: Yes

VIII. RELATED CASE(S) IF ANY

DATE: 1/7/2013

IX. DIVISIONAL ASSIGNMENT (Civil L.R. 3-2): SAN FRANCISCO/OAKLAND

Figure 3.2 Federal court Civil Cover Sheet

of preset categories for cases. The filing party must select one (and only one) of those categories, namely, the category which the filing party or attorney for that party determines best describes the case.

These categories are called Nature of Suit (NOS) codes.

With the caveat that most of the states have their own version of a Civil Cover Sheet, Figure 3.2 shows a screenshot of the *federal* Civil Cover Sheet.

Note that, across the top of Figure 3.2, PACER has stamped the document number, Document 1-1, indicating that it is related to Document 1 (the Complaint).

The case number carries a number of meanings. The number 14 indicates the year, in this case 2014. The *cv* means *Civil* rather than Appellate, Bankruptcy, Criminal, or Multi-District Litigation. The 00095 means that the case was the 95th case filed in that court in that year.

The year the case was filed is self-explanatory, but note that lawsuits come flying in. This case was number 95 even though it was filed on only January 7, 2014.

As you can see from the body of the Civil Cover Sheet, the form lists all of the NOS codes that PACER used in 2014. In 2014, there were approximately 160 NOS codes. In other years, the number of NOS codes might be larger or smaller. The reason for this is that, at times, old codes may be dropped by PACER, and new ones may be added.

Note that there is only one box checked on this form, and that someone in the court clerk's office reviewed the form to ensure this. That person then circled the box, and logged it into the system. The box checked here is NOS code 442. This NOS code number 442 is the code for the Civil Rights—Employment category of cases in the Civil Cover Sheet but in PACER is called Civil Rights: Jobs.[4]

With a PACER account, login, and password, PACER can be searched by anyone using these NOS codes.[5] In fact, using the Advanced Search option, PACER can be searched by region, case number, case title, NOS code, date ranges (filed and terminated), and party names (Figure 3.3).

But as a first cut, PACER can be searched according to the tabs across the top and just below the page name of the PACER Case Locator. The tabs refer to either *All Courts, Appellate, Bankruptcy, Civil, Criminal,* or *Multi-District*[6] cases. We selected Civil for all of our searches.

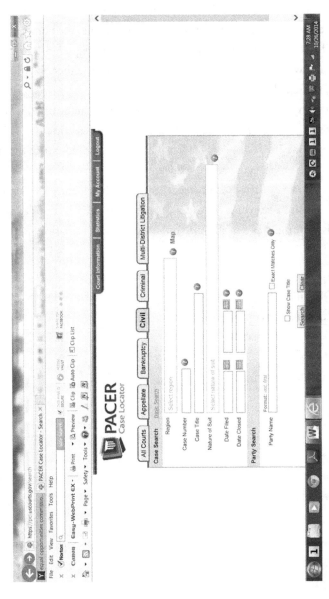

Figure 3.3 PACER's Case Locator opening screen (advanced search)

Attorneys and members of their staff almost never use or search the fields for Region, NOS code, the date ranges, or the party name. They know and use the *case number* of the case they're handling or the one they want to find, and if they've forgotten it, or don't have the number at hand, they input the case title. (When attorneys use the case number, they must follow one of PACER's formats. For the case in Figures 3.1 and 3.2, the number would be 14-00095. With a party name (either Spandow or Oracle), the search would locate the case.)

That's why the NOS code typically never enters an attorney's mind again. It's just a category the system uses to compile statistics.

But now, as our tech-savvy readers will see, we should notice that we have two levels of categorization, *Civil* and NOS code 442.

Unfortunately, further subcategories within NOS code 442 are not accessible. But according to the Equal Opportunities Employment Commission, the types of illegal employment discrimination are:

- Age
- Disability
- Equal pay or compensation
- Genetic information
- Harassment
- National origin
- Pregnancy
- Race or color
- Religion
- Retaliation
- Sex
- Sexual harassment.[7]

In a shortcoming that should be remedied, PACER does not split out these subcategories.[8]

We learned to search PACER in a different way. We used the NOS code and a date range. We added a party name when the need arose, with caveats we'll describe later.

To see how litigious we are, at least in the federal system, we used only the Date Filed category. We accessed PACER's annual data from January 1 through December 31 of each year, for the 10-year period from 2004 through 2013. Because we did not use an NOS code, PACER's output for each year was the total number of cases that were Civil in nature, including codes that are not business relevant, such as Prisoner petitions including Habeas Corpus petitions (NOS codes 463, and 510 through 560) and Freedom of Information Act cases (NOS code 895).

We found that, from start to finish over this 10-year period, the number of cases is high, but is *not* increasing at some knock-your-socks-off rate. Under the *Civil* tab in 2004, there were 284,124 cases filed. In 2013, the number of cases had risen to 305,168, an increase of 21,044 cases, a 7.41 percent increase over the 2004 figure.

We wondered about the overall 7.41 percent increase from 2004 to 2013, but found that it was not cause for alarm. For the sake of comparison, and without drawing any analogies, the annual figure for the Consumer Price Index—All Urban Consumers (All Items, 1982–1984 = 100) was 189 in 2004 and 233 in 2013.[9] The increase was 23.32 percent.

In fact, in calendar year 2014, the total number of all cases filed in the federal courts *declined* slightly from 305,168 in 2013, to 303,357. Thus, the perception that there is too much litigation is based almost entirely on having to deal with an average of about 280,000 cases every year. When the figures are this high, even a small percentage decrease seems like no relief at all, while a small percentage increase may seem intolerable.

So, during this 10-year time period, there was a rise in the number of cases but it was not explosive. The caseload went up-and-down over time, and we cannot say why it fluctuated. The lowest number of cases was filed in 2005, when 249,805 cases were filed. The highest number was in 2010, when 347,234 cases were filed.

Our spreadsheet data is shown in Figure 3.4.

Graphically, this data looks like that shown in Figure 3.5.

After we had worked our way through PACER, we found confirmation. By including cases removed to federal court from state court, Law Professor Patricia W. Hatamyar Moore found a 9 percent increase since 1986.[10] In a law review article on the subject, Professor Moore

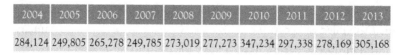

2004	2005	2006	2007	2008	2009	2010	2011	2012	2013
284,124	249,805	265,278	249,785	273,019	277,273	347,234	297,338	278,169	305,168

Figure 3.4 PACER data: total annual civil cases filed

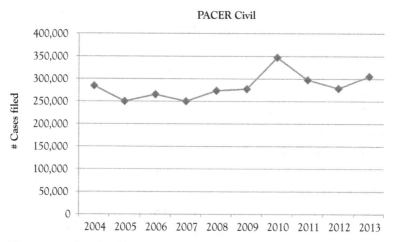

Figure 3.5 Graph of PACER data in Figure 3.4

wrote, "[s]ince 1986, instead of an *explosion* of the civil docket, the opposite has occurred: if not quite an implosion, at least stagnation."[11] We had read the data the same way.

Taken as a whole, there were about 2.8 million civil cases (2,827,193 cases to be exact) *filed* in PACER during the 10 years from 2004 through 2013.[12]

The average caseload for that 10-year period is 282,719. Around that average, the caseload since 2004 has bounced over and under that figure.[13]

Next, we looked at the NOS details. We used PACER's filter to examine the NOS codes during this 10-year period. That was instructive. In order to focus on the most frequently chosen NOS codes, we arbitrarily drew a line at 9,999 cases *per code*. When we found a year in which 10,000 cases were filed in a particular NOS code, we took note. There were 12 NOS codes at that level.

So, first, we show these NOS code numbers and PACER's description for each of them (where P.I. means Personal Injury), where at least

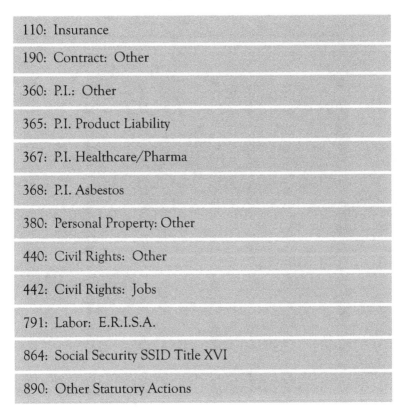

110: Insurance

190: Contract: Other

360: P.I.: Other

365: P.I. Product Liability

367: P.I. Healthcare/Pharma

368: P.I. Asbestos

380: Personal Property: Other

440: Civil Rights: Other

442: Civil Rights: Jobs

791: Labor: E.R.I.S.A.

864: Social Security SSID Title XVI

890: Other Statutory Actions

Figure 3.6 High frequency NOS codes

10,000 cases were filed in just one of the 10 years we were considering (Figure 3.6).[14]

The significance of these 12 NOS codes (out of a 10-year average of 166 codes) is that, while we chose the 10,000-cases threshold arbitrarily, these 12 categories alone accounted for about 38 percent (37.96 percent, to be more precise) of all the cases. Since we were looking for only a handful of NOS codes on which to focus first, the data was beginning to guide us.

Next, we wanted to see a trend, and for that we needed to build a time series. We wondered how often these categories reached the 10,000 threshold? Once? More than once? In the spreadsheet shown in Figure 3.7, we show the NOS codes and descriptions from the list given in Figure 3.6, and the number of cases filed in each code for each of the 10 years between 2004 and 2013.

	2004	2005	2006	2007	2008	2009	2010	2011	2012	2013
110 Insurance			12,430	13,314		10,918				11,268
190 Contract: Other	13,998	13,240	13,376	13,228	13,851	15,337	14,108	13,751	12,882	11,742
360 P.I.: Other			12,685							
365 P.I. Product Liability	30,785	23,475	28,194	14,508	22,648	16,275	20,928	18,496	23,151	44,766
367 P.I. Healthcare										10,400
368 P.I. Asbestos			10,640	15,147	33,494	35,334	46,115	38,564		
380 Personal Prop.: Other	20,083									
440 Civil Rights: Other	18,818	15,155	14,790	14,552	14,758	15,023	15,077	15,731	15,967	15,028
442 Civil Rights: Jobs	18,818	15,529	13,555	12,713	12,993	13,726	14,598	14,834	14,307	12,346
791 Labor: E.R.I.S.A.	11,145	10,343								
864 Social Security										10,214
890 Other Statutory	17,158	12,082	13,393	14,057	11,553	11,875	11,487	11,625	11,627	11,006

Figure 3.7 Caseload and NOS time series data

Using boldface, we have highlighted the four categories in which more than 10,000 cases were filed in *each* of the 10 years: 190 (Contract: Other); 365 (Personal Injury Product Liability); 442 (Civil Rights: Jobs); and 890 (Other Statutory).

Now, what can we say about the data for NOS code 368, P.I.: Asbestos (which means Personal Injury: Asbestos)? Referring back to our tabulation, we have highlighted NOS code 368, and underlined its data to make it stand out. Our first observation is that, in the early years we studied, the number of cases did not rise above 10,000. There were fewer than 10,000 cases in 2004 and 2005. But then the numbers begin to build up and they did so rather dramatically.[15] In 2006, Asbestos cases registered above 10,000 in 2006, with 10,640 cases. The number of cases increases like a fever for each year of the next five years until the number reaches a peak in 2010, with 46,115 cases.

We have to pause here for a comment. If some stock market analyst somewhere had been tracking these Asbestos cases and seen this trend, such a person might have been increasingly sour on the companies that were hit hardest. We'll see an example when we get to the Fortune 500 sector of Engineering and Construction.

But in 2011, the number declined to 38,564. Our hypothetical analyst, if he or she were a bit daring, might have suspected that the fever had broken. And that person would have been right, because the number of cases dropped below 10,000 in both 2012 and 2013. Time will tell whether this new trend will hold. In 2014, it did. The number declined to only 276 cases.

The more important point here is that there is market-relevant information in the data pertaining to litigation caseload. But so far as we know, no one has been looking.

Three other codes stand out, and one of them is not in the spreadsheet.

First, NOS code 367, Personal Injury Healthcare or Pharmaceutical, is interesting. In 2007, there were seven cases filed. In 2008, only three cases were filed. Similarly, in 2009, 10 cases were filed, but in 2010, the number moved up, but only to 13.

But after 2010, the number of cases filed in NOS code 367 began to move up more dramatically: in 2011, 1,115 cases were filed; in 2012, the number went much higher, to 7,359; and then in 2013, for the first time, the caseload moved over 10,000. The trend-line is upward, if not flaring up like Asbestos. Why? We do not know. We call attention only to the trend.

Second, we see the reverse in NOS code 152, Contracts: Recovery: Student Loans. Here are the numbers: In 2000, there were 22,201 cases; in 2001, 10,113; and in 2002, 4,212. In the following years, the cases fell to about 2,500. But in 2011, the trend did not hold and the number of cases filed jumped up to 4,328. But then in the next two years, the trend was reestablished. The number of cases filed declined to 2,176 in 2012 and to 1,930 in 2013, the lowest number since 2000. Here is an example of a *decreasing* trend.

Next, NOS code 380, Personal Property: Other is worth noting. The number of cases filed in that code rose above our (arbitrary) 10,000 case threshold in only one year, 2004. But the caseload does not reach that level again. Perhaps the code description is too vague. We could be wrong, but we doubt that this NOS code will be particularly relevant going forward.

Similarly, we note that NOS code 864, Social Security, SSID, Title XVI, appears only in 2013.

But what about the last category in our spreadsheet, Code 890: Other Statutory? We had to discount this category because it is an aggregation of many statutes, not just one.

Overall, we may have known *qualitatively* that, as a society, we battle with each other under the rule of law. Generally speaking, we use brief-cases and words, not firearms. But we now have caseload data to conclude that quantitatively, yes indeed we are a litigious society.

But while the federal numbers are high, and the overall trend is up, we find that the trend is not increasing exponentially, and is somewhat choppy.

It may take an economist to provide a better explanation than we can. It may be that our propensity to reach for a lawsuit is higher when the economy is turning from good to bad, and vice versa, but with a lag. That is, when the economy is turning from good to bad, then, after a lag, litigation increases. Similarly, when the economy is turning from bad to good, plaintiffs are, after some time, less dissatisfied, and so they are more reluctant to start a lawsuit.

Also, there may be shifts in the mix of lawsuit categories. For example, if there are shifts in lower cost litigation matters (if there is such a thing) to a higher cost category of litigation, such as patent litigation (NOS code 830), then the business community may perceive a higher level of financial pain *even if the overall caseload remains the same.*

However, our suppositions are only our best guesses, and we leave the matter of explaining litigation swings to others.

Still, this exploration was illuminating, and so the results also became actionable business intelligence. We used the data to decide which NOS codes to focus on first. It would be inefficient to pay attention to all or even most of the NOS code categories. The phrase for tackling so many NOS codes right off the bat is *boiling the ocean*, and that's not a good strategy.

So, for the purpose of moving forward, we focused on just three other categories, the three codes for which we used boldface in Figure 3.7, excluding NOS code 890. They are:

- NOS code 190, Contract: Other
- NOS code 365, Personal Injury Product Liability
- NOS code 442, Civil Rights: Jobs

These three categories were the only categories where at least 10,000 cases were filed in each of the 10 years we considered. Of just these three, the categories ranked as follows:

NOS code 365, P. I.: Product Liability   243,226
NOS code 442, Civil Rights: Jobs   143,419
NOS code 190, Contract: Other   135,513

We also found that we could see which companies in a specific industry sector had a caseload competitive advantage (that is, fewer cases) or disadvantage, as well as the mix of cases with which they were burdened.

For example, we looked at the Fortune 500 industry sector of Engineering and Construction companies. In this industry, *Fortune* lists 10 companies, but we'll discuss only the top two companies by caseload: Fluor and CH2M Hill. In Figure 3.8, we show both companies by their Fortune 500 rank by revenue, as *Fortune* does. Then we used PACER to compile their history histories in connection with NOS code 368 (Asbestos) and NOS code 442 Civil Rights: Jobs.

Engineering	2013 F500 Rank	2004	2005	2006	2007	2008	2009	2010	2011	2012	2013	Totals
Fluor	110											
Cases		116	335	1,855	2,498	13,471	5,172	952	104	80	96	24,679
368		44	275	1,817	2,406	12,420	3,346	312	36	17	27	20,700
442		9	14	4	2	13	0	23	0	7	7	79
CH2M Hill	415											
Cases		7	6	16	15	30	1,680	483	96	72	9	2,414
368		0	0	0	0	0	0	0	0	0	0	0
442		1	0	0	1	2	3	4	2	0	5	18

Figure 3.8 Caseload, NOS data for two engineering companies

We noticed immediately that Fluor was sued 24,679 times, to a much greater extent than other companies in the engineering sector of the Fortune 500. Overall, CH2M Hill was sued 2,414 times, a distant second.

On the other hand, Fluor ranked 110 on the Fortune 500, while CH2M Hill was ranked 415.

For these two NOS codes, we can see the problem areas by inspection. Let's look more closely at Fluor and CH2M Hill in the years where the number of cases exceeded a thousand, from 2006 to 2009. In 2006, Fluor was burdened with 1,855 cases, but further research tells us that 1,817 of them were in NOS code 368, which, as we have seen, is the code for Asbestos cases.

In the other years, Fluor's results are similar. In 2007, there were 2,498 cases, but 2,406 of them were Asbestos cases. In 2008, there were 13,471 cases, but 13,420 cases were, again, Asbestos cases. In 2009, out of a total of 5,172 cases, 3,346 cases were Asbestos cases.

Since Fluor was remarkable, we looked still further into the data. In 2009, we found that 73 were *other* cases (meaning we did not examine the categories in which they were filed, except for NOS code 442); while the remaining 1,753 cases were NOS code 365 (Product Liability) cases.

As for CH2M Hill, in 2009, there were zero NOS code 368 (Asbestos) cases, so we also went further. In 2009, out of 1,680 total cases, we saw that 1,573 cases were filed in NOS code 365 (P. I.: Product Liability).

From the data, it appears that Fluor was beset with the Asbestos *virus* that hit so many other companies between 2006 and 2009.

But CH2M Hill, notwithstanding the fact that it had the second highest number of cases filed against it within this sector, had *zero* Asbestos cases. On the face of it, CH2M Hill was not hit with Asbestos claims. However, that conclusion depends on whether a plaintiff correctly coded the Civil Cover Sheets. If every plaintiff or plaintiff's counsel used NOS code 365 for an Asbestos claim, when a more specific code was available, then the coding is wrong.

But that's a stretch. The odds are against 1,573 case filers, when they filled out the Civil Cover Sheet, making the same mistake of overlooking NOS code 386 for Asbestos in favor of NOS code 365 for Product Liability.

Still, it seemed odd that only one engineering company would attract so many Asbestos cases, while other engineering companies attracted product liability cases, but far fewer and sometimes zero Asbestos cases. It could be that Fluor's *projects* were fundamentally different. Analysts who specialize in this sector might know; we confess that we do not.

For Fluor, for the years 2011 to 2013, the number of Asbestos cases declined dramatically to 36, 17, and 27, respectively.[16] Fluor's Asbestos fever seems to have broken, at least insofar as the number of *cases filed* is concerned.

Still, a speculative implication is not hard to conjure. Although Fluor may have been aware that it was being hit with Asbestos cases, and that the number was increasing dramatically for a number of years before abating, the other companies in this sector were likely unaware of it. Unaware of an ability to make a comparison, they might have counted themselves lucky to have avoided the Asbestos nightmare, perhaps without knowing that two competitors were living it. But had they known of Fluor's and CH2M Hill's Asbestos troubles, the other companies might have seen a path toward exercising a competitive advantage over one or the other, or both. We don't know, and we did not investigate. So we can only say that having more information *might* have inspired different initiatives or courses of action.

But we believe that viewing litigation caseload in this way—by industry sector—is yet another innovation.

To solidify this point, we constructed another industry sector analysis. For this exercise, we chose the next sector on *Fortune's* list: Entertainment.

In this example, we present the data for all of the companies. As one might expect, Asbestos is not a problem. Instead of focusing on two codes, we chose only one, NOS code 442 (Civil Rights: Jobs). There were only seven companies in this sector. Two companies had an overall competitive *dis*advantage, Viacom (with 27,006 cases filed) and CBS (with 12,026 cases filed).

The Entertainment sector data appears in Figure 3.9.

Without a doubt, looking at the last 10 years, Viacom is the caseload leader, which is not a good thing. However, the data also shows that the current trend is down, from 4,969 in 2009, and then from 2010 to 2013 down to 503 to 284 to 201 to 149 in those years.

What happened? As before, we have no answer and only demonstrate here that this sort of analysis *may* be market-relevant information, meaning relevant to investors, employees, and even competitors.

CBS runs second in the number of cases, but notice that Time Warner has been involved in far more employment discrimination cases (285) than all of the other companies in the sector combined (172).

Entertainment	2013 F500 Rank	2004	2005	2006	2007	2008	2009	2010	2011	2012	2013	Totals
Walt Disney	66											
Cases		52	53	38	40	27	44	40	44	33	37	408
442		12	5	0	5	1	9	2	5	3	5	47
News Corp.	91											
Cases		0	0	0	5	2	0	1	1	1	2	12
442		0	0	0	1	0	0	0	0	1		2
Time Warner	105											
Cases		139	112	267	173	148	155	152	208	141	134	1,629
442		55	22	17	30	24	42	32	26	14	23	285
CBS	186											
Cases		700	552	699	1,118	2,125	2,703	2,197	993	528	411	12,026
442		24	1	6	4	7	10	9	14	6	2	83
Viacom	198											
Cases		4,305	2,903	1,715	2,425	9,552	4,969	503	284	201	149	27,006
442		9	6	1	4	1	4	0	1	4	6	36
CC Media	407											
Cases		0	0	1	1	2	4	0	0	3	6	17
442		0	0	0	0	1	0	0	0	0	2	3
LiveNation	439											
Cases		0	2	49	20	21	27	36	56	31	24	266
442		0	0	1	0	0	0	0	0	0	0	1

Figure 3.9 Caseload, NOS data for the Entertainment sector

Why? What is it about the culture at Time Warner that produces more discrimination cases in the sector than all the others combined? Is Time Warner even cognizant of this dubious distinction? Does the marketplace know? Would the information make a difference in Time Warner's stock price? We cannot say.

As we have said, we are not aware that anyone has previously answered the *just how litigious are we* question in a quantitative way, except for Professor Moore, or looked at this question by industry sector, much less made an effort to compare the average *cost* of the litigation burden to profits or losses.

Should the market take litigation burden into account? We think the answer is yes. The Big Data is there, and we have been letting it speak.

To summarize, the PACER caseload data told us how litigious we were (in federal court) from the beginning of 2004 to the end of 2013; that the annualized growth rate is, overall, positive but low; and revealed which NOS codes exceeded 10,000 cases each year during that 10-year time frame.

We also learned which NOS codes were prominent (most frequent). That information allowed us to focus on two of the top three NOS codes (Product Liability and Civil Rights: Jobs), instead of trying to boil the ocean.

Finally, we could see in the Engineering and Entertainment sectors how these two NOS codes were impacting which companies over time. By looking at the data this way, we could see which companies either had a litigation caseload advantage or disadvantage, not only by the caseload totals but also by the caseload *types*.

The fact that in-house counsel and C-suite executives may be unaware of this sort of caseload data is telling, but telling of what? Each business enterprise, no doubt, currently quantifies the *number* of lawsuits, and perhaps tracks their type, but that's an individual experience, and (to our knowledge) no one has aggregated this data or quantified the *cost* of a litigation caseload *per case*.

We had to acknowledge that the market does not speak in terms of *caseload*. The market speaks in terms of dollars.

So we had to go there, and that's next.

CHAPTER 4

Preserving Assets

Companies and business organizations around the country have complained, year after year, about the cost of litigation, but to our knowledge no one's ever done the calculations. What's the cost of an average commercial (not automobile accident) lawsuit, per case, per company, and per year? As a percentage of costs, or profits, or losses? What's it worth to prevent that lawsuit?

This chapter presents a combination of data sets[1] to derive an average *litigation cost* per case, and the other metrics we've mentioned. The first results were staggering, so we present those knock-your-socks-off numbers up front:

- The *cost* of commercial tort litigation for the 10 years from 2001–2010 (rounded) is about $1.6 *trillion*.
- The number of federal and state lawsuits of the same type for the same 2001–2010 period is about 4 *million*.

These two numbers, reduced by 15 percent, as we will explain, show that the average *cost* of a commercial tort lawsuit in the United States is about $350,000; yes, $350,000 *per case*.

Now we need to explain how we came to this astounding conclusion.

In order to persuade the market that there was Big Value in having a litigation early warning system, we wanted to see if we could persuade ourselves that such a system was worth creating. In other words, we knew *what* an early warning system was supposed to do, and how to achieve our goal of finding *hot words* in unstructured text (as we explain in later chapters), but we didn't know *why* anyone would be persuaded to want it.

In other words, what was the business case?

In 2014, we realized that lawsuit cost data had existed for many years, and that Towers Watson (NYSE: TW) had published the data. So we began our analysis with the 2011 Update of the United States Tort Cost Trends published by TW. TW has been publishing its compilation of these costs since 1985. The 2011 Update was the 15th such study. It provided us with litigation cost data for a 10-year period, from 2001 to 2010. Since the 2011 Update, TW has not published another study, so the 2010 data is TW's most recent compilation of the *cost* of litigation to the business community.

By *costs*, TW was describing: (1) benefits paid or expected to be paid to third parties (losses), (2) defense costs (attorneys' fees), and (3) administrative expenses. We adopted TW's definition.

TW reported *personal* and *commercial* tort costs separately, noting that personal torts consisted primarily of automobile accidents. We weren't interested in automobile accidents because they were more likely the result of negligent conduct by individuals in the spur of the moment. We knew that we have very little chance of being able to detect such negligence by looking at internal communications. Since we were interested in tort cases alleged against businesses, we did not consider *personal* tort costs. We also ignored nonmonetary cases such as Freedom of Information Act (FOIA) lawsuits.

Instead, we focused only on the cost of *commercial tort litigation*, which includes medical malpractice (professional negligence) cases. We wanted to see that data over time. So we plotted the TW commercial tort cost data for the period 2001–2010, and we show it in Figure 4.1.

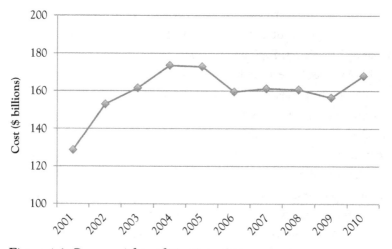

Figure 4.1 Commercial tort litigation costs

As Figure 4.1 indicates, the total costs of commercial tort costs ranged *annually* between a low of just over $120 billion and almost as high as $180 billion. As we noted at the beginning of this chapter, the total *commercial tort costs* for the 10-year period from 2001 through 2010 is almost $1.6 trillion, yes, with a *t*—trillion.

More specifically, but equivalently, the 10-year cost was $1,595 billion. Since TW reported that its cost information came from A.M. Best, whose data comes from the insurance industry, and SNL Financial, we assumed that insurance companies and at least one financial institution were giving TW data for both federal *and* state court losses, attorneys' fees, and administrative costs. Since the average cost *per case* would be $1,595 billion divided by the number of commercial tort cases in both the federal and state courts for the same 2001–2010 period, we turned to the federal and state court tort caseload databases.

We knew that federal and state caseload databases existed, and that the federal database existed for the same 10-year period from 2001 through 2010. With this and state court data, we endeavored to estimate the average *per case* cost of a commercial tort lawsuit and derive the commensurate savings to businesses if such lawsuits could be prevented.

Figure 4.2 displays our estimate of the number of nonauto tort cases filed in the federal and state courts for the same 2001–2010 period.

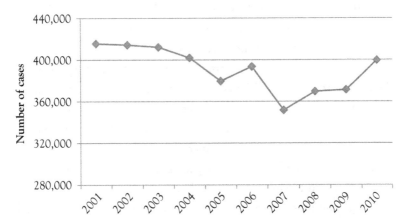

Figure 4.2 Estimated number of commercial tort cases, federal and state

Figure 4.2 requires some explanation. First, we caution that mixing federal and state court data is admittedly a database mashup and is far from being an exact science. For example, there are many federal commercial tort categories that have no state court parallel.

In addition, one might think that the definition of case categories in the Civil Cover Sheets of both federal and state court cases would be at least broadly consistent. Not so. We learned from the state court data provided by The National Center for State Courts (NCSC)[2] and the NCSC's Court Statistics Project (our sources for aggregated state court caseload data) that the descriptions in the Civil Cover Sheets used by the various *states* are not even consistent with each other.

Thus, we learned that the federal and state systems have not coordinated with each other to align their caseload categories. To the extent possible, this oversight should be corrected.

So Figure 4.2 displays the best estimate we could present with the data we had. We constructed that data in two stages.

First, we accessed the federal database, Public Access to Court Electronic Records (PACER) to obtain caseload data for the federal system.

Using PACER, we aggregated all of the *Civil* cases filed, but we *excluded* cases under the headings that are not likely to involve commercial torts, such as Bankruptcy, Contract, Federal Tax Suits, Forfeiture or Penalty, Prisoner Petitions, Real Property, Social Security, State Reapportionment, Deportation, Other Statutory Actions, Freedom of Information Act, Arbitration, Administrative Procedure Act or Review or Appeal of Agency Determination, and Constitutionality of State Statutes.

We did not include multidistrict lawsuits.

But we included all of the cases filed under the headings of Civil Rights, Labor, Property Rights (copyright, patent, and trademark), Torts, and the following specific statutes or categories: the False Claims Act, Antitrust, Banks and Banking, Commerce, Racketeer Influenced and Corrupt Organizations, Consumer Credit, Cable and Satellite TV, Securities or Commodities or Exchange, Agriculture Acts, the Economic Stability Act, and Environmental Matters.

Using only these categories of cases, we determined that the total number of cases filed in PACER from 2001 through 2010 added up to 1,248,327.

In order to determine the number of state court cases filed, we turned to the NCSC databases and located a spreadsheet called *Tort Trend in General Jurisdiction Courts*, which covered the same period of time as the TW cost data, namely, from 2001 through 2010.

We determined, however, that three adjustments to the state court data were appropriate. Our first adjustment was to accept the data *as is*, despite the NCSC caveats that some of it was incomplete or preliminary.

Second, we found that the data pertained to only 40 states plus Puerto Rico. In order to be consistent with PACER's data, which is national in scope, we had to account for the 10 states for which data was missing: Georgia, Illinois, Louisiana, Montana, Rhode Island, South Carolina, South Dakota, Vermont, Virginia, and Wisconsin. We did so by making an adjustment according to population.

According to U.S. census figures, these 10 states constituted about 16 percent of the total U.S. population on April 1, 2000 (15.9 percent) and on April 1, 2010 (15.8 percent). Thus, the caseload data for the 40 states was only 84 percent of the total. To estimate the total for all states, we divided the 40-state figure by 84 percent.

Next, after learning that some states reported automobile accidents separately, we asked the NCSC for that information. Since TW had noted that automobile accidents *predominate* in *personal* tort cases, we wanted to subtract the automobile torts in order to match apples with apples as best we could. The NCSC was accommodating, but had data for only four states: Arizona, Colorado, Connecticut, and Florida. We compared the auto tort data with the total data for each of these four states, and we found that approximately 56 percent of the total caseload was due to automobile accidents. The nonauto accident caseload was approximately 44 percent. Accordingly, we made the assumption that 44 percent of the caseload consisted of commercial tort lawsuits. Since we had no data allowing us to believe that the drivers in these states were different from the drivers in any other state, we multiplied the NCSC's 50-state *Tort Trend* data by 44 percent.

Using these criteria, we estimated the total nonauto tort caseload from 2001 through 2010 for all states plus Puerto Rico to be 2,660,609 cases.

Then we added the federal caseload figure of 1,248,327 to the state court caseload figure of 2,660,609. The total was 3,908,936 cases, which, given the uncertainties, we rounded to 3.909 million cases, and then rounded again. The idea of 4 million lawsuits over a 10-year time frame is enough to give anyone a headache.

Before moving on, we call attention to the fact that the overall caseload trend line was downward from 2001 to 2005, but that after an upward spike in 2006 and another downward shift in 2007, the caseload has increased in each of the next three years.

This data suggests at least two possible implications. The first implication is that the rise in caseload coincides with the onset of the Great Recession in 2008. We question whether such a rise is an early indicator of a downturn in the economy. Perhaps an economist will make this case, or debunk it. We only raise the question.

A second implication is that, since the caseload began increasing in 2007–2008, the rise could also be interpreted to mean that neither *tort reform* nor corporate *compliance* programs were able to keep the tide of litigation on its previous downward track. Is there any demonstrable cause-and-effect relationship between such campaigns or programs and caseload swings?

Setting those comments to the side, we had both cost and caseload data for the same 10-year period and could compute the average commercial tort litigation cost per case. To do so, we divided $1,595.2 billion (TW's *cost* for the 10-year period from 2001 to 2010) by 3.909 million cases (our estimate of the number of federal and state nonauto tort cases in the same period).

The result was easy to see in a back-of-the-envelope way, because 1,595.2 was almost 1,600, while 3.909 was almost four, so we expected the numbers would turn out to be around 400; and we knew that a billion was a thousand times more than a million, and so we expected something like $400,000.

We found that the overall average cost per case was $408,084, or approximately $408,000.

In Figure 4.3, we plot the average cost per case for each of the years and the trend.

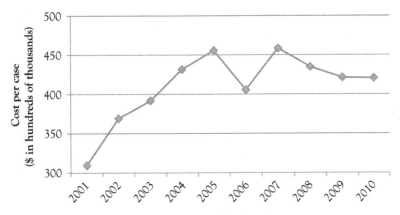

Figure 4.3 Estimated cost per case, federal and state

We note that our *per case* cost of $408,000 is an average over 10 years' time, and, given all of the adjustments, a rough *global* average at that. However, our graph shows that the cost per case was taking off like a rocket from 2001 through 2005. No wonder the call for *tort reform* had some traction.

But given the adjustments we had to make, and to be conservative, we reduced our estimated average *cost per case* result by 15 percent, to $346,871, which we then rounded to $350,000. Our result means that if an enterprise is able to avoid a *single* lawsuit, that enterprise (or its insurer) can rationally estimate that it has avoided approximately $350,000 in *costs*.

This $350,000 *per case* number is hardly insignificant. The result *is* significant for several reasons. First, we are unaware of any other *per case* calculation. Since this *per case* figure was unavailable, this *per unit* cost of doing business has been relatively unexamined over the years, if at all.

Second, our result means that if an enterprise prevents only *three* average commercial tort lawsuits per year, a little over $1 million in net profit would *stay* on the bottom line. Litigation costs are not part of anyone's cost of goods sold. Thus, a successful effort to avoid only *three* average cases would preserve approximately $1 million in net profits, or reduce losses by just as much.

Were we happy with this result? Yes and no. We were happy to get a result and be able to explain how we got there. But there were estimates and compromises along the way. We backed off by 15 percent, but we had plucked that number out of the air, just to be conservative. How could we know that we were right, or even roughly right?

We had no answer to that question until we saw a damages study that was reported by Lex Machina in 2014.[3] Lex Machina specializes in providing its customers with data pertaining to Intellectual Property (IP) litigation, meaning patents, trademarks, and copyright litigation. In July of 2014, Lex Machina published a result for damages in patent cases, but for an even longer time frame, from 2000 to 2013. For that time period, Lex Machina reported a *median* damages figure of $372,000 per case.[4]

We cheered. At least in the patent litigation silo, Lex Machina had, at least in part, corroborated our research.

Of course, patent litigation is a narrower field than commercial tort lawsuits, and the range of damages is likely broader, from zero to billions of dollars in a handful of cases. And the Lex Machina patent litigation damages figure is not a mean, which is the *sum* of all values divided by the *number* of all values; it's a median, indicating only that as many litigants won more than $372,000 as won less than that.[5]

Still, the Lex Machina result is supportive of the result we calculated.

Then, on May 6, 2015, Lex Machina announced its first Trademark Litigation Report,[6] reporting, among other metrics, that trademark attorneys had filed more than 24,000 trademark cases from 2009 through the first quarter of 2015, and that those cases resulted in more than $9 billion in cumulative damages. We did the math: $9 billion divided by 24,000 is the same as $9 million divided by 24, which is $375,000 per case.

Now, while we hope that it is our global calculation that our readers will notice, we knew that there were more granular metrics that were already being tracked. These metrics provide a solid business case for electronic *preventive law* analytics, and pertain to the operation of the corporate Legal Department:

- The number of cases;
- The cost of settlements and verdicts;
- The cost of outside counsel and eDiscovery vendors; and
- The costs of administration.

But because each Legal Department is governed by a budget, has a certain history of litigation, and has paid the costs of verdicts and settlements, attorneys' fees, eDiscovery vendors, and administrative costs, success with *less litigation* would mean that, after a reasonable amount of time (for example, two to four years):

- The number of lawsuits per year would be less than the base year;
- The losses (verdicts and settlements) stemming from litigation would level out or decrease;
- The cost of outside litigation counsel would level out or decrease;
- The cost of outside eDiscovery vendors would level out or decrease; and
- The overall *spend* by the Litigation Department would level out or decrease.

Wouldn't that be great? After all, our primary goal is to decrease the Legal Department's *spend*, increase the corporation's bottom-line profits, and let the enterprise be more productive with the money it earns, so that it can provide better products and/or services for its customers and better returns for its shareholders.

We end this chapter by making this contention: There is *quantifiable* Big Value in less litigation.

CHAPTER 5

Protecting Leadership and Other Intangibles

In the last chapter, we recounted our considerable effort to demonstrate that a litigation early warning system could preserve net profits of over $1 million for every three lawsuits it avoids, per year.

But in Chapter 4, we didn't mention the other metrics we see—the intangible ones—and it is useful to lay them out. These metrics are less tangible than dollars and cents, but they are no less real. With a litigation early warning system, in-house counsel can also help the enterprise find the distractions that reveal friction and dysfunctions, and the circumstances that impair productivity. The recognition and avoidance of those circumstances provides the enterprise with still further benefits:

- Higher productivity due to fewer distractions for management and other employees;
- More opportunities for optimization by identifying and addressing dysfunction;
- Preservation of valuable commercial relationships;
- Early revelation of potential health and safety threats to employees and customers; and,
- A new way to protect enterprise leadership when it needs it the most.

All of these benefits are valuable, but the last two points are particularly significant. The early revelation of health and safety threats implies fewer plaintiffs and fewer lawsuits. The clear implication is that fewer customers and employees will die, be seriously injured, or have their rights violated. Their families, and society as a whole, would benefit.

The last point is that the corporation's *leadership* also benefits. But before we get to the details of this last intangible on the list, one idea here is that all sorts of complaints are worth knowing about, not just a formal Complaint in a lawsuit. To put it bluntly, the opportunity for prevention can be actionable business intelligence for a company's *and* for society's benefit *if* someone is listening to, and learning from, customer and employee complaints.

That notion may seem odd. It's tough to listen to complaints. But the truth is that complaints are valuable, and they come in many forms. For example, in some cases customers are telling the enterprise, in call center complaints and warranty claims, where a future disaster is brewing. Enterprises should pay heed when someone says that the circumstances amount to a *lawsuit waiting to happen.*

So customers present early warnings, and so do employees. Employees present the enterprise with two kinds of complaints. In their e-mails and instant messages, they are telling the enterprise how to improve. They are making suggestions. But they are also telling the enterprise where they see friction or, worse, dysfunction.

In our view, business executives devote too little attention to this, but we don't blame them. It's our nature to avoid hearing the bad news. Even if we should pay attention to bad news before we pay attention to good news, we always seem to want to hear about the good news and never the bad news.

But by identifying and preventing potential legal problems, for example, the system can also improve an enterprise's standing with government or regulatory entities, and the public at large, potentially upholding the corporation's ethics and preserving, if not enhancing, corporate credibility and goodwill.

No one gets fired if they increase profits and the enterprise's credibility at the same time.

And, better still, from the financial standpoint, is the greater likelihood that the next bet-the-company litigation or public relations disaster might be avoided. The benefit of preventing such a high-stakes situation is far greater than just preserving $350,000 by avoiding the average case. The value of avoiding extremes that can damage a corporation's reputation is huge. Such outliers represent hits to profitability in the multimillion and low billion dollar range, and can deflate a company's stock and capitalized value. So any system with a shot at spotting and avoiding such outcomes is potentially extremely valuable.

In fact, from a broader perspective, lowering the overall risk *profile* of the enterprise is arguably even more beneficial in the long run than lowering the enterprise's legal costs next year.

And perhaps just as vital to overall productivity, if there were fewer instances of *litigation holds*, the technology designers and engineers, and so many other employees, will be just so *grateful*. They are unfamiliar with disputes, lawsuits, eDiscovery (especially depositions), and they would suffer less stress if they were thrown such curves less frequently. When the corporation is forced to send out a notice to such folks to tell them that they are the custodians of potentially relevant evidence, and must preserve their data (in a document called a legal *hold* notice), they worry. The notice is a shock to their systems. Their productivity goes down.

Moreover, following Jim Groton's lead, if friction develops, for example, with one of the company's suppliers or joint venture partners, the friction could be defused before a disagreement becomes a dispute, or worse. Then some of the company's previously formed (and treasured) business relationships won't get pushed to the breaking point.

We have traveled a long way yet again. We have discussed both tangible metrics in the previous chapter and intangible benefits so far in this one. We have answered a key question: Can a litigation early warning system help the enterprise protect its assets? The answer is yes.

But we have saved the best for last. Now we come to another benefit of a different kind. It is one of the most important realizations we made on our journey. We shift to this key question: Can a litigation early warning system provide a significant benefit to the enterprise's *leadership*?

More specifically, can an early warning system protect the control group executives? Can it protect the Directors and Officers? The answer is yes.

Here's why. The enterprise, by intentionally installing a system to find litigation threats and to be proactive about them, protects itself from the downside and cost of governmental (regulatory) investigations. These investigations sometimes go nowhere, but they can also lead to criminal charges. In a white-collar criminal case, the company's leadership faces not only the distraction, but the stress and cost of having to defend against a threat to one's *liberty*.

But what if an early warning system is installed by the Legal Department and used in good faith? First of all, over time, an enterprise with a *preventive* system in place would gain a higher standing with regulatory agencies. In other words, it seems to us that by accepting and practicing *preventive law*, and by being proactive, the Board of Directors and the control group executives are building credibility with both consumers and regulators. Credibility is valuable. Attorneys who are familiar with a trial before a jury will likely support our contention that, in that context, credibility is more valuable than anything else.

That's good, and certainly of interest, but an early warning system promises to do even more than that.

So let us describe why we trumpet this particular intangible benefit. In the case of the *United States v. Lauren Stevens*, Lauren Stevens was indicted in the wake of a government accusation that her company, GlaxoSmithKline (NYSE: GSK), was selling Wellbutrin, an anti-anxiety compound, as a weight-loss compound. The Food and Drug Administration (FDA) had not approved Wellbutrin for that use. Such off-label sales were illegal.

So subpoenas were issued and Ms. Stevens took charge of responding to them. She engaged outside counsel, hired experts, and relied on their recommendations. To make a long story short, when the government was not satisfied with GSK's response, Ms. Stevens was accused of obstructing justice. She was an officer of the company and an Associate General Counsel, and she was *indicted*.

GSK stood by Ms. Stevens. Eventually, after two trial proceedings and millions of dollars, the District Court *dismissed* the indictment, stating that the case should not have been brought in the first place. The ruling was based on the lack of evidence showing *a specific intent to do harm*. More specifically, as the court in Ms. Stevens's case put it, "[g]ood faith reliance on the advice of counsel, when proven, *negates the element of wrongful intent ...* ."[1]

Remember that phrase: *negates the element of wrongful intent*. So when the Legal Department uses a system to investigate, find, and avoid or prevent potential harm to customers and employees, the *enterprise* is relying in good faith on the *advice of counsel*. The enterprises' Directors and Officers (the Ds and Os) would be directing the attorney employees to do the right thing, which is always the right thing to do. The system may save buckets of money for the business and its stakeholders, but it also displays the exact opposite of the mental state the government would have to prove in a white collar criminal case. The government has to prove a specific intent to *do* harm; the preventive system we've been suggesting is proof of a specific intent to *avoid* harm.

Now let's look at the other side of the beach ball. Without such a system in place, what would a savvy plaintiff or prosecutor argue? The answer is obvious: it's the *asleep at the switch* argument. On occasion, the plaintiff or the government has an even better argument: that whoever held the purse-strings was too interested in profitability to be diligent and put short-term profit first, ignoring the likely adverse consequences to others.

Why is the first argument obvious? Because we've seen it before: a lack of control can jeopardize the leadership and the shareholders alike. A lack of *financial* controls opens the door to fraud by employees. A lack of *data security* opens the door to the loss of personally identifiable information, trade secrets, and more. So a *lack* of control in key areas can be devastating.

The second argument is also obvious. There are a few famous instances where enterprises knew that their product was harmful and reckoned that the cost of litigating a few death or serious injury cases would be less expensive than a recall or a costly change to the product or to the production line.

Thus, this last *intangible* benefit on our list is one of our most important realizations. A *preventive law* approach *negates the element of wrongful intent*. This virtue of a preventive law *early warning system* is that it may alleviate the biggest financial downside and the worst personal experience any member of a corporation's leadership could ever experience.

CHAPTER 6

Introducing the Litigation 100

Now let us look more closely at the biggest companies of our nation and find out who really needs a system to prevent litigation. After all, caseload information is not typically disclosed.

We begin this chapter by announcing yet another innovation: the Litigation 100.

The Litigation 100 is new, but the companies in our ranking are the familiar ones and are the same as the first 100 companies in the Fortune 500.

We'll call that collection of top companies, which *Fortune* ranks by revenue, the Fortune 100. Our Litigation 100 ranking is new, but easy to understand. The question the Litigation 100 answers is simple: Of the 100 largest corporations in the United States *by revenue* in any given year, as ranked by *Fortune*, how do these same 100 companies rank according to their litigation caseload?[1]

Right off the bat, we confess that our new ranking is imperfect. We are not considering state court cases. We are putting our ranking together using only federal court cases. Why? The answer is that we focus on the federal litigation database, Public Access to Court Electronic Records (PACER), because it is the only litigation database with national scope, just as the companies on which we focus are (at least) national in scope.

It is likely that all of our readers will be familiar with the Fortune 500. We can find the famous Fortune 500, of course, at *Fortune* magazine's website.[2] *Fortune* parses its list in many ways: by revenue, as we have noted, but also by industry (in over 70 sectors), headquarter state, and by various financial benchmarks.

But we believe that one important benchmark has been ignored: litigation caseload. How do these same companies rank in connection with litigation-related risk? That ranking has not previously been available, in any format of which we are aware.

So, with this chapter, we introduce the Litigation 100. We aim to shed some light on the extent to which each corporation is engaged in federal court litigation in a specific year. If litigation is toxic, as they say, a little sunshine will be a fine disinfectant.

But we are also mindful that the Litigation 100 is our construct, and has not been vetted by others. So, to avoid being too close to present-day market conditions, we accessed the Fortune 500 in 2013, and selected only the top 100 companies; that is, the 2013 Fortune 100. We present the 2013 Fortune 100 by Revenue, as *Fortune* does, but with a new twist: We also show our best estimate of the number of cases filed in PACER during the calendar year 2012.[3]

Ranked by revenue (1 = most)	Fortune 100	# cases filed 01/01/2012– 12/31/2012
1	Walmart and Wal-Mart	1,635
2	Exxon Mobil	560
3	Chevron	142
4	Phillips 66	17
5	Berkshire Hathaway	41
6	Apple Inc. and Apple Computer	164
7	General Motors	233
8	General Electric	704
9	Valero Energy	7
10	Ford Motor	395
11	AT&T	581
12	Fannie Mae	287
13	CVS Caremark	85
14	McKesson Corp	244
15	Hewlett-Packard and Hewlett Packard	123
16	Verizon Communications	490
17	United Health Group	245
18	J.P. Morgan Chase and J. P. Morgan Chase	142
19	Cardinal Health	166

20	IBM and International Business Machines	111
21	Bank of America	3,880
22	Costco Wholesale	101
23	Kroger	122
24	Express Scripts Holding	22
25	Wells Fargo	3,766
26	Citigroup	476
27	Archer-Daniels-Midland and Archer Daniels Midland	38
28	Procter & Gamble and Procter and Gamble	44
29	Prudential Financial	63
30	Boeing	110
31	Freddie Mac	117
32	AmerisourceBergen	25
33	Marathon Petroleum	15
34	Home Depot	454
35	Microsoft	146
36	Target	579
37	Walgreen	335
38	American International Group and AIG	279
39	INTL FCStone and FCStone	6
40	Metropolitan Life and MetLife	972
41	Johnson & Johnson	23,669
42	Caterpillar	104
43	PepsiCo	116
44	State Farm Insurance	1,273
45	ConocoPhillips and Conoco Phillips	632
46	Comcast	248
47	WellPoint	40
48	Pfizer	1,164
49	Amazon & Amazon.com	381
50	United Technologies	85
51	Dell Computer and Dell Financial and Dell Inc.	65
52	Dow Chemical	129
53	United Parcel Service	180

(Continued)

Ranked by revenue (1 = most)	Fortune 100	# cases filed 01/01/2012– 12/31/2012
54	Intel Co	41
55	Google	219
56	Lowes and Lowe's	346
57	Coca-Cola and Coca Cola	67
58	Merck	2,591
59	Lockheed Martin	210
60	Cisco Systems	33
61	Best Buy	160
62	Safeway Corp and Safeway Grocery and Safeway Inc.	42
63	Federal Express and FedEx	350
64	Enterprise Products Partners	98
65	Sysco	36
66	Walt Disney	33
67	Johnson Controls	64
68	Goldman Sachs Group	119
69	CHS Inc.	1
70	Abbott Laboratories	104
71	Sears Holdings	107
72	E. I. du Pont and E.I. du Pont	130
73	Humana	103
74	World Fuel Services	34
75	Hess Corp and Hess Energy	127
76	Ingram Micro	3
77	Plains All American Pipeline	4
78	Honeywell International	328
79	United Continental Holdings	24
80	Oracle	72
81	Liberty Mutual Insurance Group	1,077
82	HCA Holdings	14
83	Delta Air Lines	109
84	Aetna	459
85	Deere	31
86	Supervalu	57

87	Sprint Nextel	81
88	Mondelez	3
89	New York Life Insurance	73
90	American Express	187
91	News Corp	23
92	Allstate Fire and Allstate Inc.	477
93	Tyson Foods	41
94	Massachusetts Mutual Life Insurance	75
95	Tesoro	16
96	Morgan Stanley	450
97	TIAA-CREF	40
98	General Dynamics	76
99	Phillip Morris International	8
100	Nationwide	82
	Totals	54,833

Before we go on, a few explanations are in order. First, we should explain why we compared the 2013 Fortune 100 companies with PACER data from 2012. For this, we quote from *Fortune's* statement concerning its own methodology. For the 2013 Fortune 500 list, Fortune stated, "Data shown are for the fiscal year ended on or before January 31, 2013. Unless otherwise noted, all figures are for the year ended December 31, 2012."[4]

Accordingly, we used the party names for the calendar year in which cases were *filed*, beginning January 1, 2012 and ending December 31, 2012. The number of cases filed against a company is an indicator of risk, and we assumed that when a Fortune 100 company is a party to a case when it was filed, it was far more likely than not to be a defendant.

In the process, we discovered that plaintiffs or their counsel don't always use a company's official name and sometimes spell it in unusual ways. We made this discovery because PACER is a database and is literal. If a party spelled a company's name incorrectly, PACER lists the case that way. For example, Wal-Mart is sometimes spelled Walmart. The company is the same but PACER lists both names, which means that if we are searching for Wal-Mart we will miss cases where the company's name is spelled correctly or differently. We found the same to be true whenever a company name was hyphenated, as in Hewlett Packard and Hewlett-Packard, and in Archer Daniels Midland and Archer-Daniels-Midland.

We adjusted for this as best we could. When we identified alternative spellings for a company name, we included the case totals for both versions of the name. In the listing we called the Fortune 100, we showed the alternatives as and when we found them.

Similarly, a search in PACER for J.P. (no space between the J and P) Morgan will return a different set of cases than if the search is for J. P. Morgan (with a space between the J and the P.) We found the same anomaly for E.I. du Pont and E. I. du Pont. Once we found this oddity, we counted the cases for both versions, and brought the issue to the attention of PACER. PACER responded by agreeing to permit a wildcard within the first three characters, which doesn't help in all cases, of course, such as in the Walmart example.

Parties will also sometimes use acronyms, but PACER is not currently equipped with an acronym library. Thus, PACER does not equate AIG with American International Group, GE with General Electric, GM with General Motors, or IBM with International Business Machines. We searched for both, a party's name and its acronym, in order to have any sense that we were accurately counting a company's caseload.

Also, we noted that a search for the word *Apple*, by itself, was over-inclusive. We had to search for Apple Computer and Apple Inc. in order to exclude cases that involved other companies with *apple* in their names.

And we hasten to say that the results we report are understated. First, our count does not include state court cases. We also did not consult reports that public companies must file in the database of the Securities and Exchange Commission (such as 10-K reports), and so our tabulation might be short to the extent that we also missed subsidiaries. Moreover, we strongly suspected that each company would consider its actual case-load metric to be confidential information, and so we also did not contact the companies to ask them for this information. The caseload data comes only from PACER.

Finally, we stress that the Litigation 100 ranking is inverse to the financial rankings to which we are accustomed. For characteristics like revenue, asset, and shareholder equity, *more* is better. A company with the highest amount of revenue would be ranked the highest.

But the highest amount of litigation indicates the highest amount of potential risk for payouts in settlements and verdicts; the highest potential risk for incurring attorneys' fees paid to outside counsel; the highest potential risk for having to pay expert witness fees and expenses; the highest potential for eDiscovery vendor costs; and so on. Thus, for all of the costs pertaining to any filed lawsuit, *less* litigation is better. The company with the lowest caseload should be ranked first, not last.

But we know that readers will be more interested in seeing which company had the highest caseload. The Litigation 100 reflects this. Our Litigation 100 ranks the same 100 companies listed in the 2013 Fortune 100, but puts the companies with the *highest* number of lawsuits at the top of the list.[5]

With all that said, we believe that the Litigation 100 presents market-relevant results.

For example, market analysts might take the Litigation 100 list still further, and we list three examples of how they might do so. First, there should be a time series for each company. Is the caseload data trending up or down? In light of other information, what does the trend mean?

Second, companies in the same industry sector may expect to be hit with lawsuits of a somewhat similar nature. With the Litigation 100, each company can measure itself against other companies in the same industry sector. If there is a significant caseload disparity over time, a company with less litigation should enjoy a competitive advantage over a company with more. A significant disparity may impact investor confidence and even share prices.

Third, during the due diligence period of a merger or acquisition transaction, the amount of a target's caseload may reveal something about the target company's culture, its tolerance for litigation risk, and perhaps a need for improvement in areas such as regulatory compliance or data security. Every purchase agreement should have a provision for a price adjustment once the acquiring enterprise has direct access to the target's information systems. Where would we look? The acquiring company may know the names of the target's due-diligence team. Why not look at their e-mails during the due diligence period?

The Litigation 100 will make sense once you see it. In the next chapter, we will present the Litigation 100 by converting the caseload to the *cost* of that caseload. After that, we will present our estimate of cost *as a percentage of profits* where the company had profits, and as a percentage of losses if the company suffered losses. But first, here is the Litigation 100:

Ranked by most cases filed *against* (100 = most)	Litigation 100	# cases Filed 01/01/2012– 12/31/2012
100	Johnson & Johnson	23,669
99	Bank of America	3,880
98	Wells Fargo	3,766
97	Merck	2,591
96	State Farm Insurance	1,273
95	Walmart	1,635
94	Pfizer	1,164
93	Liberty Mutual Ins. Group	1,077
92	Metropolitan Life	972
91	General Electric	704
90	ConocoPhillips	632
89	AT&T	581
88	Target	579
87	Exxon Mobil	560
86	Verizon Communications	490
85	Allstate	477
84	Citigroup	476
83	Aetna	459
82	Home Depot	454
81	Morgan Stanley	450
80	Ford Motor	395
79	Amazon.com	381
78	Federal Express	350
77	Lowes	346
76	Walgreen	335
75	Honeywell International	328

74	Fannie Mae	287
73	AIG	279
72	Comcast	248
71	United Health Group	245
70	McKesson Corp	244
69	General Motors	233
68	Google	219
67	Lockheed Martin	210
66	American Express	187
65	United Parcel Service	180
64	Cardinal Health	166
63	Apple Inc.	164
62	Best Buy	160
61	Microsoft	146
59	Chevron	142
59	J.P. Morgan Chase	142
58	E. I. du Pont	130
56	Hess Corp & Hess Energy	127
56	Dow Chemical	129
55	Hewlett-Packard	123
54	Kroger	122
53	Goldman Sachs Group	119
52	Freddie Mac	117
51	PepsiCo	116
50	IBM	111
49	Boeing	110
48	Delta Air Lines	109
47	Sears Holdings	107
45	Caterpillar	104
45	Abbott Laboratories	104
44	Humana	103
43	Costco Wholesale	101
42	Enterprise Products Partners	98
41	United Technologies	85
40	CVS Caremark	85
39	Nationwide	82

(Continued)

Ranked by most cases filed *against* (100 = most)	Litigation 100	# cases Filed 01/01/2012– 12/31/2012
38	Sprint Nextel	81
37	General Dynamics	76
36	Mass. Mutual Life Ins.	75
35	New York Life Insurance	73
34	Oracle	72
33	Coca-Cola	67
32	Dell Inc.	65
31	Johnson Controls	64
30	Prudential Financial	63
29	Supervalu	57
28	Procter & Gamble	44
27	Safeway	42
24	Berkshire Hathaway	41
24	Intel Co	41
24	Tyson Foods	41
22	WellPoint	40
22	TIAA-CREF	40
21	Archer-Daniels-Midland	38
20	Sysco	36
19	World Fuel Services	34
17	Cisco Systems	33
17	Walt Disney	33
16	Deere	31
15	AmerisourceBergen	25
14	United Continental Holdings	24
13	News Corp.	23
12	Express Scripts Holding	22
11	Phillips 66	17
10	Tesoro	16
9	Marathon Petroleum	15
8	HCA Holdings	14
7	Phillip Morris International	8
6	Valero Energy	7

5	INTL FCStone	6
4	Plains All American Pipeline	4
2	Ingram Micro	3
2	Mondelez	3
1	CHS Inc.	1
	Totals	54,833

As the numbers stand, the differences between the 2013 Fortune 100 and the 2012 *Litigation* 100 are striking. We begin with Walmart. Walmart ranked #1 on the 2013 Fortune 100 list for revenues, but was #95 on the Litigation 100. Why? Could Walmart do better? Or is Walmart simply too big for 1,635 lawsuits to even matter?

Johnson & Johnson is another matter altogether. When you scan the Litigation 100 list, this company stands out. In the Litigation 100, Johnson & Johnson ranks in position #100, with involvement in a whopping 23,669 cases. By itself, Johnson & Johnson's caseload is about 43 percent of the total 54,833 federal court cases filed against *all* of the other companies in the Litigation 100 combined. Can this be right?

Johnson & Johnson would know best, but the data from other years says yes. For these same 100 companies in 2011, one year *before* the results we report above, the total number of Cases Filed was 49,533. Of this total in 2011, Johnson & Johnson was named in 12,970 cases, which is about 26 percent of the total. In 2013, one year *after* the data we report above, the total number of cases filed against these same companies declined from the 2012 level of 54,833 cases to 50,461 cases, but Johnson & Johnson was named in 21,266 cases, or about 42 percent of the total.

Thus, Johnson & Johnson's 2012 levels were higher than they were in 2011, both in terms of the number of cases in which it was named, and as a percentage of total number of cases; but they were about the same, in both respects, in 2013.

Now, of course, no decisions should be made from this data alone, especially since the data may not state the actual truth in several ways. First, caseload information for other countries is, to the best of our knowledge, unavailable. Second, we note that our estimate does not include state court cases. The number of state court cases filed for the period

2001–2010 was 2,660,609, but required more than one adjustment, and turned out to be a little over twice as many cases as the federal court caseload for the same time frame.[6]

So the federal court caseload is only a proxy for the complete picture.

Moreover, the source of our federal court caseload data is PACER, and we have seen that PACER records a party's name in the way that the plaintiff uses it in the complaint, and we cannot be sure that we accounted for all of the variations.

Last, we know of no database that aggregates both federal *and* state caseloads by party name. And the Nature of Suit codes are, as between the federal and state court systems, *not* synchronized. So our Litigation 100 ranking may have merit, but we may be looking at the data only through a very scratchy lens. While there may be ways to sharpen the picture in the future, this is the best we can do for now.

Nevertheless, we contend that this information can be useful to decision-makers outside the companies, such as analysts and shareholders; and those within it, such as members of the Board of Directors, and by company leaders such as CEOs, compliance officers, and the leaders of the Legal Departments.

In our next chapter, and despite the shortcomings we have acknowledged, we will build on the Litigation 100. We will present two other firsts: the first-ever calculation of the *cost* of commercial tort litigation *per company* per year, and the first-ever commercial tort litigation cost per company per year *as a percentage of profits or losses.*

CHAPTER 7

Litigation Cost as a Percentage of Profits and Losses

In the previous chapter, we explained how we derived the Litigation 100. In a nutshell, the Litigation 100 reranked the first 100 companies in 2013 Fortune 500 by the number of federal court cases to which each company was a party in 2012.

Besides the caseload rankings, the larger point is that we can now estimate the cost of commercial tort litigation *per company* per year.

After a downward adjustment, the litigation cost per case turned out to be about $350,000. Here, we multiply the caseload data by the cost per case, and so extend the Litigation 100 to show each company's estimated (federal court only) total commercial tort litigation cost in 2012.

2013 rank (100 = most cases filed)	Litigation 100	# Federal cases in 2012	Est. 2012 commercial litigation costs = # cases filed × $350,000 per case (in thousands)
100	Johnson & Johnson	23,669	8,284,150
99	Bank of America	3,880	1,358,000
98	Wells Fargo	3,766	1,318,100
97	Merck	2,591	906,850
96	State Farm Insurance	1,273	445,550
95	Wal-Mart	1,635	572,250
94	Pfizer	1,164	407,400

(Continued)

2013 rank (100 = most cases filed)	Litigation 100	# Federal cases in 2012	Est. 2012 commercial litigation costs = # cases filed × $350,000 per case (in thousands)
93	Liberty Mutual Ins. Group	1,077	376,950
92	Metropolitan Life	972	340,200
91	General Electric	704	246,400
90	ConocoPhillips	632	221,200
89	AT&T	581	203,350
88	Target	579	202,650
87	Exxon Mobil	560	196,000
86	Verizon Communications	490	171,500
85	Allstate	477	166,950
84	Citigroup	476	166,600
83	Aetna	459	160,650
82	Home Depot	454	158,900
81	Morgan Stanley	450	157,500
80	Ford Motor	395	138,250
79	Amazon.com	381	133,350
78	Federal Express	350	122,500
77	Lowes	346	121,100
76	Walgreen	335	117,250
75	Honeywell International	328	114,800
74	Fannie Mae	287	100,450
73	AIG	279	97,650
72	Comcast	248	86,800
71	United Health Group	245	85,750
70	McKesson Corp	244	85,400
69	General Motors	233	81,550
68	Google	219	76,650
67	Lockheed Martin	210	73,500
66	American Express	187	65,450
65	United Parcel Service	180	63,000
64	Cardinal Health	166	58,100
63	Apple Inc.	164	57,400

62	Best Buy	160	56,000
61	Microsoft	146	51,100
59	Chevron	142	49,700
59	J.P. Morgan Chase	142	49,700
58	E. I. du Pont	130	45,500
56	Hess Corp & Hess Energy	127	44,450
56	Dow Chemical	129	45,150
55	Hewlett-Packard	123	43,050
54	Kroger	122	42,700
53	Goldman Sachs Group	119	41,650
52	Freddie Mac	117	40,950
51	PepsiCo	116	40,600
50	IBM	111	38,850
49	Boeing	110	38,500
48	Delta Air Lines	109	38,150
47	Sears Holdings	107	37,450
45	Caterpillar	104	36,400
45	Abbott Laboratories	104	36,400
44	Humana	103	36,050
43	Costco Wholesale	101	35,350
42	Enterprise Products Partners	98	34,300
41	United Technologies	85	29,750
40	CVS Caremark	85	29,750
39	Nationwide	82	28,700
38	Sprint Nextel	81	28,350
37	General Dynamics	76	26,600
36	Mass. Mutual Life Ins.	75	26,250
35	New York Life Insurance	73	25,550
34	Oracle	72	25,200
33	Coca-Cola	67	23,450
32	Dell Inc.	65	22,750
31	Johnson Controls	64	22,400
30	Prudential Financial	63	22,050
29	Supervalu	57	19,950
28	Procter & Gamble	44	15,400
27	Safeway	42	14,700

(Continued)

2013 rank (100 = most cases filed)	Litigation 100	# Federal cases in 2012	Est. 2012 commercial litigation costs = # cases filed × $350,000 per case (in thousands)
24	Berkshire Hathaway	41	14,350
24	Intel Co	41	14,350
24	Tyson Foods	41	14,350
22	WellPoint	40	14,000
22	TIAA-CREF	40	14,000
21	Archer-Daniels-Midland	38	13,300
20	Sysco	36	12,600
19	World Fuel Services	34	11,900
17	Cisco Systems	33	11,550
17	Walt Disney	33	11,550
16	Deere	31	10,850
15	AmerisourceBergen	25	8,750
14	United Continental Holdings	24	8,400
13	News Corp.	23	8,050
12	Express Scripts Holding	22	7,700
11	Phillips 66	17	5,950
10	Tesoro	16	5,600
9	Marathon Petroleum	15	5,250
8	HCA Holdings	14	4,900
7	Phillip Morris International	8	2,800
6	Valero Energy	7	2,450
5	INTL FCStone	6	2,100
4	Plains All American Pipeline	4	1,400
2	Ingram Micro	3	1,050
2	Mondelez	3	1,050
1	CHS Inc.	1	350

As this spreadsheet shows, our data indicates that only one company, CHS Inc., experienced less than $1 million in litigation cost, while three companies—Wells Fargo, Bank of America, and Johnson & Johnson—experienced litigation costs in excess of $1 billion.

According to *Fortune*, each of these three companies was profitable, but what was the litigation cost as a percentage of profits or losses? Because *Fortune* reports data for each company's profits (92 were profitable) and losses (the other eight), we can make these calculations too.

Lit. 100 rank		# Federal cases in 2012	Est. lit. costs ($ thousands)	2012 profits ($ thousands)	Litigation costs as a % of profits	2012 losses ($ thousands)	Costs as a % of losses
100	Johnson & Johnson	23,669	8,284,150	10,853,000	76.33		
99	Bank of America	3,880	1,358,000	4,188,000	32.43		
98	Wells Fargo	3,766	1,318,100	18,897,000	6.98		
97	Merck	2,591	906,850	6,168,000	14.70		
96	State Farm Insurance	1,273	445,550	3,159,200	14.10		
95	Wal-Mart	1,635	572,250	16,999,000	3.37		
94	Pfizer	1,164	407,400	14,570,000	2.80		
93	Liberty Mutual Ins. Group	1,077	376,950	829,000	45.47		
92	Metropolitan Life	972	340,200	1,324,000	25.69		
91	General Electric	704	246,400	13,641,000	1.81		
90	ConocoPhillips	632	221,200	8,428,000	2.62		
89	AT&T	581	203,350	7,264,000	2.80		
88	Target	579	202,650	2,999,000	6.76		
87	Exxon Mobil	560	196,000	44,880,000	0.44		
86	Verizon Communications	490	171,500	875,000	19.60		
85	Allstate	477	166,950	2,306,000	7.24		
84	Citigroup	476	166,600	7,541,000	2.21		

83	Aetna	459	160,650	1,657,900	9.69		
82	Home Depot	454	158,900	4,535,000	3.50		
81	Morgan Stanley	450	157,500	68,000	231.62		
80	Ford Motor	395	138,250	5,665,000	2.44		
79	Amazon.com	381	133,350			3,900,000	3.42
78	Federal Express	350	122,500	2,032,000	6.03		
77	Lowes	346	121,100	1,959,000	6.18		
76	Walgreen	335	117,250	2,127,000	5.51		
75	Honeywell International	328	114,800	2,926,000	3.92		
74	Fannie Mae	287	100,450	17,220,000	0.58		
73	AIG	279	97,650	3,438,000	2.84		
72	Comcast	248	86,800	6,203,000	1.40		
71	United Health Group	245	85,750	5,526,000	1.55		
70	McKesson Corp	244	85,400	1,403,000	6.09		
69	General Motors	233	81,550	6,188,000	1.32		
68	Google	219	76,650	10,737,000	0.71		
67	Lockheed Martin	210	73,500	2,745,000	2.68		
66	American Express	187	65,450	4,482,000	1.46		
65	United Parcel Service	180	63,000	807,000	7.81		
64	Cardinal Health	166	58,100	1,069,000	5.43		

(Continued)

Lit. 100 rank		# Federal cases in 2012	Est. lit. costs ($ thousands)	2012 profits ($ thousands)	Litigation costs as a % of profits	2012 losses ($ thousands)	Costs as a % of losses
63	Apple Inc.	164	57,400	41,733,000	0.14		
62	Best Buy	160	56,000			441,000	12.70
61	Microsoft	146	51,100	16,978,000	0.30		
59	Chevron	142	49,700	26,179,000	0.19		
59	J.P. Morgan Chase	142	49,700	21,284,000	0.23		
58	E. I. du Pont	130	45,500	2,788,000	1.63		
56	Hess Corp & Hess Energy	127	44,450	2,025,000	2.20		
56	Dow Chemical	129	45,150	1,182,000	3.82		
55	Hewlett-Packard	123	43,050			12,650,000	0.34
54	Kroger	122	42,700	1,496,500	2.85		
53	Goldman Sachs Group	119	41,650	7,475,000	0.56		
52	Freddie Mac	117	40,950	10,982,000	0.37		
51	PepsiCo	116	40,600	6,178,000	0.66		
50	IBM	111	38,850	16,604,000	0.23		
49	Boeing	110	38,500	3,900,000	0.99		
48	Delta Air Lines	109	38,150	1,009,000	3.78		
47	Sears Holdings	107	37,450			930,000	4.03

45	Caterpillar	104	36,400	5,681,000	0.64	
45	Abbott Laboratories	104	36,400	5,962,500	0.61	
44	Humana	103	36,050	1,222,000	2.95	
43	Costco Wholesale	101	35,350	1,709,000	2.07	
42	Enterprise Products Partners	98	34,300	2,419,900	1.42	
41	United Technologies	85	29,750	5,130,000	0.58	
40	CVS Caremark	85	29,750	3,876,900	0.77	
39	Nationwide	82	28,700	748,500	3.83	
38	Sprint Nextel	81	28,350			4,326,000	0.66
37	General Dynamics	76	26,600			332,000	8.01
36	Mass. Mutual Life Ins.	75	26,250	1,114,600	2.36	
35	New York Life Insurance	73	25,550	1,333,200	1.92	
34	Oracle	72	25,200	9,981,000	0.25	
33	Coca-Cola	67	23,450	9,019,000	0.26	
32	Dell Inc.	65	22,750	2,372,000	0.96	
31	Johnson Controls	64	22,400	1,226,000	1.83	
30	Prudential Financial	63	22,050	469,000	4.70	
29	Supervalu	57	19,950			1,040,000	1.92
28	Procter & Gamble	44	15,400	10,756,000	0.14	
27	Safeway	42	14,700	596,500	2.46	

(Continued)

Lit. 100 rank		# Federal cases in 2012	Est. lit. costs ($ thousands)	2012 profits ($ thousands)	Litigation costs as a % of profits	2012 losses ($ thousands)	Costs as a % of losses
24	Berkshire Hathaway	41	14,350	14,824,000	0.10		
24	Intel Co	41	14,350	11,005,000	0.13		
24	Tyson Foods	41	14,350	583,000	2.46		
22	WellPoint	40	14,000	6,255,500	0.22		
22	TIAA-CREF	40	14,000	2,060,000	0.68		
21	Archer-Daniels-Midland	38	13,300	1,223,000	1.09		
20	Sysco	36	12,600	1,121,600	1.12		
19	World Fuel Services	34	11,900	189,300	6.29		
17	Cisco Systems	33	11,550	8,041,000	0.14		
17	Walt Disney	33	11,550	5,682,000	0.20		
16	Deere	31	10,850	3,064,700	0.35		
15	AmerisourceBergen	25	8,750	719,000	1.22		
14	United Continental Holdings	24	8,400			723,000,000	1.16
13	News Corp.	23	8,050	1,179,000	0.68		
12	Express Scripts Holding	22	7,700	1,312,900	0.59		
11	Phillips 66	17	5,950	4,124,000	0.14		
10	Tesoro	16	5,600	743,000	0.75		

9	Marathon Petroleum	15	5,250	3,389,000	0.15
8	HCA Holdings	14	4,900	1,605,000	0.31
7	Phillip Morris International	8	2,800	8,800,000	0.03
6	Valero Energy	7	2,450	2,083,000	0.12
5	INTL FCStone	6	2,100	15,000	14.00
4	Plains All American Pipeline	4	1,400	1,094,000	0.13
2	Ingram Micro	3	1,050	305,900	0.34
2	Mondelez	3	1,050	3,028,000	0.03
1	CHS Inc.	1	350	1,260,600	0.03
	Totals		54,833		

As is obvious, some of these percentages are not trivial. The top 10 companies with the highest litigation cost as a percentage of profits were:

1. Morgan Stanley (231.62 percent)
2. Johnson & Johnson (76.33 percent)
3. Liberty Mutual Ins. Group (45.47 percent)
4. Bank of America (32.43 percent)
5. Metropolitan Life (25.69 percent)
6. Verizon Communications (19.60 percent)
7. Merck (14.70 percent)
8. State Farm Insurance (14.10 percent)
9. Valero Energy (14.0 percent)
10. Aetna (9.69 percent)

The data also told us that some companies that ranked high in caseload, and so were in the bottom 50 of the Litigation 100, had *low* litigation costs as a percentage of profits. According to the data, the reason is plain to see: These companies had high levels of profits.

Only one company (Valero) ranked high on the Litigation 100 (at 6th because of its low level of cases) but also high (9th) on the Top 10 list of companies with a high cost as a percentage of profits. The reason is again obvious: Valero had a low level of profits.

The worst performer was Morgan Stanley. Morgan Stanley was named as a party in 450 cases and ranked 81 on the Litigation 100. At an average of about $350,000 per case, Morgan Stanley's estimated litigation cost in 2012 was $157,000,000. Yet, according to *Fortune*, Morgan Stanley earned only $68,000,000. That's why its cost as a percentage of profits was 231.62 percent.

At the other end of the spectrum in the bottom 50 of the Litigation 100, Apple was a party to 164 cases and ranked significantly lower than Morgan Stanley, and had a lower estimated litigation cost of $57,400,000. But because *Fortune* reported Apple with high profits of $41,733,000,000, its litigation cost as a percentage of profits in 2012 was only 0.14 percent.

Second, in the 50 companies with the smallest caseloads (from 1 to 111 cases), 45 companies had net profits, but five companies experienced net losses. Of the 45 profitable companies, the cost of litigation ranged from a miniscule 0.03 percent of profits to 14 percent, but there was only one company that exceeded the 10 percent level. The average litigation cost as a percentage of profits was 1.4 percent.

Of the 47 profitable companies with the most litigation, the cost of litigation ranged from 0.14 percent (Apple) to 231.61 percent (Morgan Stanley), and averaged 12.32 percent.

As for the companies that suffered losses, two stand out. Best Buy ranked 62 on the Litigation 100, with a federal caseload of 162 cases, which computes to an estimated litigation cost of $57,400,000. But with a loss of $441,000,000, the litigation cost was 12.70 percent of Best Buy's losses. Accordingly, it appears that litigation was a significant component of those losses.

General Dynamics ranked higher than Best Buy on the 2013 Litigation 100 list at 37, with a litigation cost that computes to $26,600,000. But this level of litigation cost was also significant, at 8.01 percent of General Dynamics's $332,000,000 in losses.

We can take this analysis one step further and be company-specific with it. In the next example, we show that our approach works to reveal information that may be market relevant for companies that are not in the Fortune 100.

For this example, let's consider Xerox. There's no acronym for Xerox and it's unlikely that the name would be spelled with hyphens or spaces. Xerox is a well-known company and its results are reported in *Fortune's* rankings, although not in the top 100.

Xerox provides us with an opportunity to illustrate PACER's filters. We do this in two steps. First, we open PACER's Case Locator.[1] Then, on the menu bar across the top, we click Civil, and just under that menu bar, click *Advanced Search*, which opens up fields for Case Title, Date Filed, and Date Closed. The latter two permit searches within a range of start and stop dates, with the dates in a particular format.

Using that format for the Date Filed range, we input 01/01/2013 and 12/31/2013. Next, under Party Search, we input *Xerox*. A screenshot of these inputs is shown in Figure 7.1.

Next, at the bottom of the screen (middle), we click Search. Figure 7.2 is a screenshot of a portion of the output, which is indicated by the second line below the Download button.

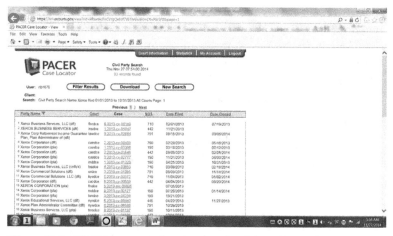

Figure 7.1 PACER screen for Xerox search parameters

Figure 7.2 PACER screen showing caseload search results

In Figure 7.2, find the Download button (between Filter Results and New Search). Just above the Download button, and below the date of the search, we see that PACER is reporting that there were 93 records found. Just below the Download button, and within the gray banner, there is a menu bar for *Party Name* (with a down-pointing triangle), *Court*, Case, *NOS*, *Date Filed*, and *Date Closed*. The data under the italicized headings (except Case) can be sorted.

To illustrate this, Figure 7.3 is another screenshot showing the same records, but sorted using the Date Filed field. We click on *Date Filed* and the triangle shifts to point downward. If we click on *Date Filed* again, the triangle reverses, points upward, and the records will be re-sorted, this time in reverse chronological order.

Next we return to our initial screenshot to illustrate the **Filter Results** button, which appears to the left of the **Download** button. Clicking on **Filter Results**, we see Figure 7.4, which shows a number of options.

Now we can sort the data by using the options in the **Filter Results** box. Once we are familiar with the Nature of Suit (NOS) codes, this

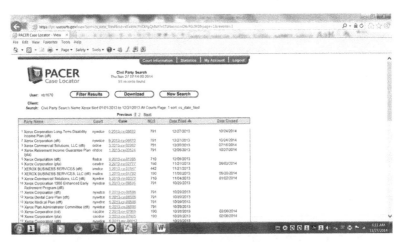

Figure 7.3 PACER *screen showing caseload results in reverse chronological order*

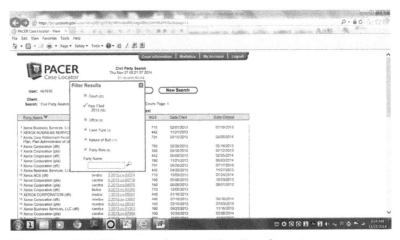

Figure 7.4 PACER *screen showing Filter Results options*

filter will be helpful as a shortcut, especially if we are interested in seeing only the NOS codes for the cases in which Xerox has been involved most frequently. So we click on the box to the left of the Nature of Suit heading, and see which of these NOS codes were chosen by plaintiffs and how many times. This is Figure 7.5.

Suppose we were interested in the time frame from 2009 through 2013, and wanted to compile a spreadsheet for which types of cases Xerox was involved most frequently in each year. We cannot sort for this information using only the Filter Results options. We have to go back to the original screen (using the *back arrow* button), and change the Date Filed start and ending ranges to 01/01/2009 and 12/31/2013.

When PACER reports the caseload for this five-year period, then we can use the Filter Results feature and the Nature of Suit filter. We discover that there are six NOS codes that account for 82.4 percent of the lawsuits in which Xerox was involved.

Let's compile the data for these six NOS codes for the period from 2009 through 2013, the total number of cases filed in each year, the average cost per case we calculated, and Xerox's reported net profits. In Figure 7.6, we discover an estimated range of litigation costs for Xerox's total *federal court* caseload as a percentage of Xerox's net profits.[2]

Now, our readers might also notice that Xerox is involved in more *breach of contract* cases than all of the other NOS categories where it

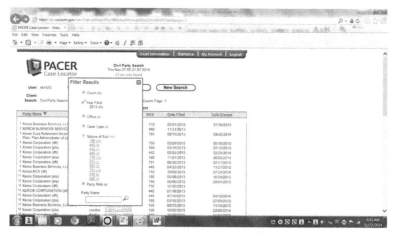

Figure 7.5 PACER screen showing NOS results

XEROX								Total Federal Caseload Only	Major NOS Total and %	Federal Caseload x $350,000 per case average ($)	Net profit per 2014 Annual Report ($)	Litigation Cost As a % of Net profit
Major NOS	190	440	442	710	791	830						
2013	37	5	7	12	13	6	93		32,550,000	1,185,000,000	2.75%
2012	54	0	12	1	6	15	104		36,400,000	1,184,000,000	3.07%
2011	21	1	4	1	7	5	53		18,550,000	1,274,000,000	1.46%
2010	30	8	6	2	7	17	83		29,050,000	591,000,000	4.92%
2009	21	4	5	0	6	1	48		16,800,000	478,000,000	3.51%
Major NOS	163	18	34	16	39	44		314 = 82%			
Five-Year Totals							381		133,350,000	4,712,000,000	2.83%
Major NOS descriptions											
190 - Breach of Contract											
440 - Civil Rights: Other											
442 - Civil Rights: Jobs											
710 - Labor: Fair Labor Standards Act											
791 - Labor: ERISA											
830 - Patent											

Figure 7.6 Spreadsheet showing Xerox caseload costs and costs as a percentage of profits

experiences slightly more litigation (163 cases) than the other five NOS codes combined (151 cases). Does this mean that Xerox frequently breaks contracts? Not necessarily. Xerox operates on an annuity model, where its contracts provide it with cash flow on a recurring basis. At times, no doubt, Xerox is a plaintiff when its customers do not pay.

Whether Xerox is a defendant or a plaintiff is an exercise we leave to the reader to obtain from the public information available from PACER. (Hint: Use the last option under Filter Results.)

Now we'd like you to notice two things: first, we repeat that our results do not take state court cases into account and so the dollar amount of litigation cost as a percentage of profits is understated; second, the litigation cost as a percentage of profits ranges from about 1.5 percent to just under five percent, and averages 2.83 percent, which likely passes the *material* threshold in the accounting sense.

This latter point may be significant. If litigation costs were lower, profits would be higher. If profits were higher, earnings per share would be higher. If earnings per share were higher, there would be upward pressure on the stock price per share.

In other words, lower litigation costs could translate into higher shareholder value. So that's a significant result. Shareholders would want that.

One of our purposes here is to teach our readers how to use PACER in ways that we had to discover for ourselves. To the best of our knowledge, what we have shown here is *not* taught in any law school *or* business school and, we believe, neither attorneys nor market analysts use PACER in the ways we have demonstrated.[3]

PART III
Preventive Law

CHAPTER 8

What Is *Preventive Law?*

The primary reason each of the first four people whom we asked to join our Board of Advisors said *yes* was that they had some connection to Professor Brown or his teachings.

So what is *preventive law*? You already know it by various sayings and proverbs:

> "It usually costs less to avoid getting into trouble than to pay for getting out of trouble."
>
> —Louis M. Brown (1909–1996)[1]

> "There is surely nothing quite so useless as doing with great efficiency that which should not be done at all."
>
> —Peter F. Drucker[2]

> "It is best to win without fighting."
>
> —Sun Tzu[3]

> "An ounce of prevention is worth a pound of cure."
>
> —Benjamin Franklin[4]

This last proverb is well known to all of us, even in our digital age. A modern application might be: Back up your computer (frequently) and hit *save* even as you're writing, even if after writing only a few pages.

There's also a saying in Latin that covers the point. The Latin is *praemonitus praemunitus,* which means forewarned is forearmed.[5]

So now we know that this notion of the value of *prevention* goes back a very long way. Today we speak in terms of preventive maintenance and preventive medicine. But law? No.

And with that, let's return to preventive *law* and its modern-day founding father, Professor Brown. His philosophy was: "The time to see an attorney is when you're legally healthy—certainly before the advent of litigation, and prior to the time legal trouble occurs."

And Professor Brown practiced what he preached, launching a program when he was President of the Beverly Hills Bar Association to give free legal advice to young couples before they were married.

Right or wrong, Nick remembers Professor Brown saying (in the 1972–1975 timeframe) that he once had a client with a fleet of trucks and had to defend the company when, at various times and under various circumstances, the truck drivers had gotten into accidents. What Professor Brown noticed, he said, was that the facts in every case had one thing in common: The drivers had gotten into these accidents when they were making left hand turns.

So should he keep on earning fees for defending these cases? No, Professor Brown said. Instead, he advised the company to have a policy that its drivers should avoid making left turns and instead make three *rights*. At the time, Professor Brown wasn't making this suggestion to save on time or gas; right turns were just safer turns to make.

In other words, Professor Brown was making a business case for *preventive law*.

Nick can't recall if Professor Brown's story pertained to United Parcel Service (UPS) or not. Probably not. But UPS has precisely this policy today. In 2008, D. Scott Davis, UPS's Chairman and former CEO, gave a speech in Los Angeles entitled *Right Turn at the Right Time*. The focus of the speech was the value of a company's reputation, but the *right turn* policy also came up. And what Scott Davis said about the *right turn* policy was this:

"We carefully map-out routes for all our drivers to reduce the number of left-hand turns they make.

Now get this: In 2007 alone, this helped us:

- Shave nearly 30 million miles off already streamlined delivery routes;
- Save 3 million gallons of gas; and

- Reduce CO_2 emissions by 32,000 metric tons, the equivalent of removing 5,300 passenger cars from the road for an entire year."[6]

So Mr. Davis was praising the policy because there were fewer miles driven and less gasoline burned.

Let's monetize Mr. Davis's figures. Suppose a mile driven by a UPS truck costs the company $0.50 per mile. Then *saving* 30 million miles saves $15 million. Now suppose that the cost of gas is only $2.50 per gallon. By these lights, saving 3 million gallons of gas saved UPS another $7.5 million.

So this Make Right Turns policy yields $22.5 million for the benefits that Mr. Davis was citing, and that means that the Make Right Turns policy is a terrific example of Professor Brown's teachings.

The point is that there is a solid business case for *preventive law*, and it's not hard to fathom.

A computer-based early warning system to avoid litigation doesn't necessarily mean there will be fewer miles driven, or lower CO_2 emissions, or even fewer collisions. But in the context of product liability cases, prevention could well mean fewer lawsuits, and that translates into a major savings in dollars, but it also means *fewer deaths and fewer injuries*.

And that's a moral high ground.

So an early warning system offers the prospect of a big *risk reduction* plus a big *cost reduction* plus a big *reputation boost*, and that's a powerful combination. What lawyer wouldn't want to deliver *that*?

CHAPTER 9

An *Early Warning System* to Prevent Litigation?

An early warning system to prevent litigation is an idea that must be taken seriously. It is an idea whose time has come. Nothing is so powerful, because our shared intuition is that such an idea is inevitable. It is the idea that litigation is not the only answer to resolving a dispute; that litigation itself can be prevented if the company is enabled by a proactive *early warning system* to prevent any damages or (at least) to mitigate them.

We focus on damages because they are a necessary element of *every* lawsuit seeking a monetary award. So it follows immediately that if there are no damages, no viable lawsuit can be filed. The operative, motivating formula on which this system stands is simple:

No Damages = No Lawsuit.

So the object is to find the lawsuit disaster while it is *still* in the making. If there's a *lawsuit waiting to happen*, let's find it while it's waiting and before the damage happens.

But can we learn from lawsuits themselves how to avoid them? Yes. Lawsuits begin with a formal document called a pleading, which is also known as a Complaint. And when Complaints are filed, they are Document 1 in most of the cases. So we need to data-mine the now-familiar Public Access to Court Electronic Records (PACER) database, but only with respect to the allegations in the Complaint to learn what facts were alleged.

But what happens *before* a Complaint is filed? What happens (usually) is that someone makes an appointment with an attorney, sits down, and after some preliminary conversation, answers questions like, "So what can I do for you? Why are you here?"

Then the facts come tumbling out and it is the attorney's job to sort out whether this prospective client has a sufficient factual basis to justify filing a lawsuit. The attorney is vetting the prospective client, of course, but another important objective is to weigh and measure the facts, to separate the wheat from the chaff.

There are several reasons for this. First, under Rule 11 of the Federal Rule of Civil Procedure, lawyers are not permitted to file lawsuits that have no merit. Second, attorneys don't make good reputations for themselves by filing, and then losing, bad cases. Conflicting *facts* make bad cases. Third, an attorney who takes on a bad case is putting himself or herself at risk. When some clients lose, they sometimes turn on their attorney and sue for malpractice.

So there are many sound reasons for believing that the facts alleged in the Complaint have been vetted.

For example, an attorney may smile when the prospective client says, "And I can prove it." To which the attorney replies, "Oh, how so?" To which the prospective client says, "I have some e-mails." And then the attorney *will* smile, and will ask to see them.

Accordingly, we may look to the factual allegations of a Complaint to find the *smoking guns*, the words and phrases (which may or may not be in an e-mail) that justified the filing of the Complaint in the first place.

We recognize that a reference to a specific e-mail or to the exact words in an e-mail may be omitted from the Complaint, because perhaps the prospective client shouldn't have copied it.

And we realize that the phrase *smoking gun* is sometimes applied to a lawsuit, as in the sense that *we'll do discovery and hope to find the smoking guns*. During the discovery phase of the litigation, the plaintiff's attorney will want to find something like five to nine documents that prove his or her client's most basic contentions. (It's hard for juries to handle more.) So we don't like the *smoking guns* phrase.

We prefer the phrase *hot words*.

The reason we prefer the phrase *hot words* is that we don't have the benefit of seeing the specific documents that a specific client may have to present to his or her prospective attorney.

But we have learned how to overcome that problem. We have realized that nothing prevents us from *aggregating* the factual allegations made in Complaints of a specific type that have been filed in the past. We do this in order to build a library of the hot words we'd like to find behind the firewall, before the damage is done.

Here are three examples of what we mean by this. The following cases were filed in early 2014, and may still be active by our publication date. It should be clear that we had nothing to do with any of these cases. We don't know the parties or their attorneys. And so we hasten to say that we are not taking sides or making any comments about the merits of any of them.

Instead, we are quoting the allegations to indicate what the plaintiff's attorney(s) thought was important, and how we can tell. For our first example, we quote portions of paragraphs 26 and 27 from the Complaint in *Spandow v. Oracle America, Inc.*[1]

> 26. In one of the e-mails Mr. Spandow wrote to his supervisor …:
> "[P***] is a 7 year Oracle employee …. I can't in good conscience, even mention $50K/$50 to him. It would be nothing short of discriminating against him based on his ethnicity/country of origin ….
>
> 27. …. Plaintiff was rebuked by …., who told Plaintiff that the salary would be "good money for an Indian."

In paragraph 26, the plaintiff's counsel is quoting from an e-mail. The sentiment phrase is "I can't in good conscience." The subject matter hot words are "discriminating against him based on his ethnicity/country of origin" and "good money for an Indian." In paragraph 27, notice that "good money for an Indian" is framed by quotation marks. We'll come back to this.

The second example is from the Complaint in *Sharma v. Atlas Aerospace, LLC.*[2] In paragraph 12, which we quote verbatim, you'll see racial hot words, also in quotation marks:

> 12. During plaintiff's employment he was repeatedly subjected to racial harassment by his supervisor. This conduct included, but is not limited to, the supervisor calling plaintiff a "sand nigger," "camel jockey," "towel head," and "turban head." The same supervisor also told plaintiff that he "looked like a terrorist" with his beard he was growing.

Our third example is from the Complaint filed by the plaintiff in *Cogburn v. Montgomery County Nursing Home Board*.[3] We quote from paragraphs 13 and 14 of the complaint:

13. L***** tells employees, "I hate pregnant women," including around A**** when she was pregnant and shortly after she had given birth and about another pregnant employee.

14. L***** tells employees who have recently given birth that they should quit work, go home, and care for their babies.

These factual allegations tell us something about attorneys when they write. When attorneys are quoting someone else, they use quotation marks, just as we all do. When attorneys want to emphasize a point, however, they may italicize it, underline it, or put it in boldface. And when they are telling the reader that some word or phrase is being emphasized, they will say so and put *emphasis added*, or, more specifically, *italics added* in parentheses.

In these ways, attorneys will point to whatever they want to stress or whatever they've added. They use these flags not only to focus the reader on the language they are stressing, but to inoculate themselves against any accusation of plagiarism.

Let's go back to those examples. In the first example, plaintiff's counsel put the phrase "good money for an Indian" in quotation marks because it was a subject matter phrase, and because he was stressing it.

In the second example, the epithets were emphasized in the same way (quotation marks), along with "looked like a terrorist." These epithets are all subject matter *hot words* and phrases.

In the third example, the attorney quoted "I hate pregnant women." In this example, the *sentiment* word and subject matter words are as close together as they can get.

With factual allegations and drafting clues like this, we can dive into the factual allegations in a sea of Complaints *in each specific NOS category*, and find the words and phrases that have launched the lawsuits of the past. In this way, we learn from the past to prepare for the future.

PART IV
Big Data and Textual ETL

CHAPTER 10

Processing Early Warning Litigation Data

Based on Professor Brown's teachings, the notion that corporations can anticipate and prevent litigation is not a new idea. As we have explained, the notion of *preventive law* has been around for decades.

Until recently, however, there were few, if any, software products that might be able to successfully implement any such notion. To explain his approach, Bill Inmon will be our voice (with very few exceptions) in Chapters 10 to 14. Because many of our readers may be unfamiliar with computer science and software, Bill will address this subject in baby steps and with lots of step-by-step graphics. Bill illustrates his presentation with graphics, but he does not use captions. To conclude his portion of our book, he'll present a Proof of Concept based on the Enron e-mails. We know that this approach may frustrate our more tech-savvy readers. We apologize in advance for that.

Here's Bill.

Gating Factors

There are many challenges to the anticipation and prevention of litigation. But the two biggest obstacles have to be the volume of data that must be examined and managed, and the fact that nearly all of the data that must be examined is in the form of text. Figure 10.1 shows that volumes of data and text are the two biggest gating factors to being able to build a system that prevents litigation:

The good news is that, with the software technology we will describe in this and the next four chapters, both of these factors can be mitigated if not overcome, although we hasten to say that perfection is too much to ask.

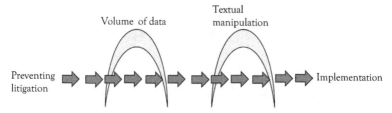

Figure 10.1

Volumes of Data

The first major challenge facing the enterprise is to deal with the volumes of data that must be processed. There are many facets to dealing with large volumes of data. But the most important aspect of dealing with large volumes of data is to embrace a technology called *Big Data*.

We are not speaking of data in the context of the fact that, in our new digital world, there is a lot of *Big Data*. Gigabytes grew to terabytes, and they grew to petabytes, and there are more 1,000-fold steps beyond that and into the future.

We mean something more practical. With Big Data, the corporation can store and process virtually unlimited amounts of data. In addition, with Big Data, the *cost* of storage and processing is much less expensive than if the same data were to be processed using technology out of the realm of Big Data.

However, Big Data has its own unique characteristics, and the attorney-analyst (who we'll just refer to as an analyst) must be aware of them.

Repetitive Data and Nonrepetitive Data in Big Data

One characteristic of Big Data is that there are two distinctly different types of data in it. The two different types of data are repetitive data and nonrepetitive data. Figure 10.2 illustrates these types of data.

At first glance, the categorization of repetitive data and nonrepetitive data may appear to be somewhat of an artificial division of data found in the world of Big Data. But the division is anything but artificial. Repetitive data is data whose occurrences (or records) are highly repetitive.

Repetitive data   Nonrepetitive data

Figure 10.2

To be clear, repetitive text is text that repeats itself, like the boiler-plate in a contract. Nonrepetitive text is text that does not repeat, such as in an ordinary e-mail. Structured data is data that has a structure imposed by a program, such as the information we input at an ATM machine. Unstructured data is data that has no perceptible structure to it.

There are many examples of repetitive data:

- Telephone call records, where the date and time of the call is recorded, the person making the call is recorded, the person to whom the call was made is recorded, and the length of the call is recorded;
- Metering data, where public utility metering data is recorded. For example, each month a meter measures how much gas and how much electricity a consumer uses;
- Machine generated data, where, for example, a manufacturer has a computer that measures output from the manufacturing process, such as temperature, chemical composition, weight, and so forth;
- Satellite meteorological data, where, during each revolution of the Earth, a satellite looks at and measures storm formation, cloud formation, temperature, and so forth; and
- Log tape data, where an entity, a corporation or a governmental agency, makes a daily log of certain activities.

With such repetitive data, the same record *format* appears over and over again. In terms of structure, and sometimes even in terms of content, the same record is recorded over and over, many, many times.

Nonrepetitive Data

Nonrepetitive data is fundamentally different from repetitive data. Some examples of nonrepetitive data include:

- E-mail: Every e-mail is different from every other e-mail. In an e-mail, people can write anything they want, including as much information or as little information as they desire to convey, all of which is outside of the structured fields identifying the sender, the intended recipient, the date, and the subject of the e-mail;
- Call center conversations: Most corporations have an 800 number to which a customer or a prospect can call the company. The person making the call can discuss anything that is on his or her mind. Like e-mails, the transcripts of such calls are examples of unstructured textual information, and they sometimes reflect a customer complaint;
- Warranty claim information: When a product malfunctions, or is perceived to have malfunctioned, customers generate a warranty claim. The information found on the warranty claim is very nonstandardized and almost always reflects a complaint; and
- Medical diagnoses: Doctors make notes regarding patients. The notes made by a doctor vary widely from doctor to doctor and from patient to patient. There is no uniformity to discern in the notes made by a doctor, even in today's world of electronic medical records.

The nature of nonrepetitive data is fundamentally different from the data contained in a repetitive format.[1]

Business Value

While there are many implications from the separation of repetitive and nonrepetitive data in Big Data, perhaps the biggest difference is in where the business value lies. Stated simply, out of the vast majority of records

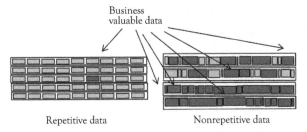

Figure 10.3

found in repetitive data, very few records have actual business value. But for nonrepetitive data, nearly every record has business value. Figure 10.3 depicts our point, this stark difference is where the business value may be found.

As an example of the difference in business value between repetitive and nonrepetitive data, consider the repetitive data of the record of telephone conversations. The record of telephone conversations is called *call level detail. Call level detail* records do not record the contents of the telephone call. Call level detail records consist only of the date, the time of the call, the length of the call, and the parties involved in the call.

In a day's time, a telephone company will create millions of call level detail records. Every time a telephone call is made, a record is created. And of all of those records created, how many will be of interest to corporations? The answer is that only a handful of records will ever be of interest to anyone. Perhaps 0.00001 percent of call record detail records are ever of any business value.

Now consider nonrepetitive records. Take warranty information as an example. Almost every warranty record will have business value. Of course, some warranty records will have great business value and some warranty records will have only a small amount of business value. But practically every warranty record will have some sort of business value. Perhaps 99.999 percent of all warranty records will have business value. Almost by definition, a customer is making a warranty claim because something went wrong. While that claim may not be good news for a corporation, there is a story in every single claim, and that story may be valuable, either by itself or in the aggregate, to a design, production, or manufacturing engineer.

Without a doubt, then, there is a stark contrast between the business value of repetitive records and the nonrepetitive records found in Big Data.

The Great Divide of Data in Big Data

We want to emphasize this point. The difference in business value between repetitive data and nonrepetitive data in Big Data is so stark that it can be said that Big Data has a *Great Divide*. Figure 10.4 shows the Great Divide of data in Big Data.

For our purposes, the Great Divide must be acknowledged. It is crucial. It is important for an analyst to know about the differences in repetitive data and nonrepetitive data in Big Data because, when the analyst wants to create (or use) an *early warning system* to prevent litigation, the analyst needs to know that it is productive to look into nonrepetitive data. That is where an analyst will find the information indicating that a potential lawsuit is incipient or *in the making*. That is where to find the signals that will set off the early warning alarms. In almost every case, it will not be productive for an analyst to look into repetitive data.

Besides looking at nonrepetitive data to find the early indications of a potential lawsuit, we need to look at text. Nearly all the early indications of a lawsuit are buried in a textual form. It is worth noting that the text of interest is the nonrepetitive type. Very little data, if any, of the repetitive type will contain any data that bears on the issue.

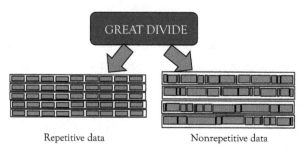

Repetitive data   Nonrepetitive data

Figure 10.4

Storing and Managing Text

Text has been around for a lot longer than computers have been around. Text can be stored in a computer in a linear fashion. When text is stored in a linear fashion, it is merely stored as a word at a time. In addition, text is inherently irregular, or unstructured. An English teacher may think that text has a structure, but a computer technician has a hard time finding the structure in text. So the unstructured nature of text is the first challenge awaiting an analyst, as seen in Figure 10.5.

Context

But there is an even greater challenge awaiting the computer analyst, and that is the challenge of obtaining the context of the text. Figure 10.6 illustrates our point that context is needed in order to make sense of text.

People take context for granted. But context is a necessary ingredient in order for text to be used for decision making. Without context, it is impossible to use text accurately for the purpose of decision making. As a simple example of the value of context, suppose two gentlemen are on a street corner and a young lady passes by. One of the gentlemen says to the other, "She's hot."

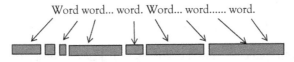

Word word... word. Word... word...... word.

The irregularity of text, the apparent lack of structure

Figure 10.5

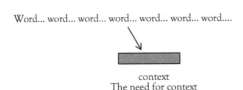

Word... word... word... word... word... word... word....

context
The need for context

Figure 10.6

Now what is being said here? One interpretation is that the lady is attractive.

Another interpretation is based on an additional fact, that the conversation is taking place in Houston, Texas, and it is taking place on a day in July, and the temperature is 98° and the humidity is 100 percent. So another interpretation is that the lady is sweating.

Yet another interpretation depends on a change of scene. Suppose the two gentlemen are doctors in a Houston ER room, and one doctor has just taken the lady's temperature or looked at her chart. She has a temperature of 104°. In this context, she is feverish.

And there are probably many other interpretations that can be made.

Note that the words—*She's hot*—do not tell us what the context is. And note further than most if not all of the context is external to the text itself. The context is determined by the location of the parties speaking (or writing) the words, the temperature, the occupation of the gentlemen, the attractiveness of the lady, and so forth. These factors are *all* external to text and have little or nothing to do directly with the text that has been spoken (or written).

Also note that there is nothing special about the words, *She's hot*. The need for context is valid for all text.[2]

In spoken text, we use voice inflection to convey context.

But in written text, we sometimes use punctuation. For example, try this sentence:

That that is is that that is not is not is that it it is

Without punctuation, the sentence makes no sense. In fact, the sentence is a well-known example of syntactic ambiguity.[3]

With punctuation alone, the sentence *does* make sense. With the commas and periods, but no additional words, the text has roughly the same meaning in two different ways:

That that is, is. That that is not, is not. Is that it? It is.
That that is, is that that is. Not is not. Is that it? It is.

But words also supply context to other words, sometimes in the sentence where the word in question is itself being used, and sometimes before or after that sentence.

There is technology that is able to read text, edit it, manipulate it, organize it into a database format, and derive the context of the text itself. The name of the technology is called *Textual ETL*. As we have noted previously, ETL stands for Extract Transform and Load.

Textual ETL is software for *textual disambiguation*. You might have become familiar with *disambiguation* if you've read a lot of *Wikipedia* entries.[4] The word *disambiguation* sounds complex but it unpacks easily enough.

The core word is *ambiguity*. For example, in *Wikipedia*, when you want to look up the word *Ford*, you get back more than one entry. Did you mean the tycoon, the car manufacturer he founded, the 38th President of the United States, or a shallow crossing on a river?[5]

So the prefix *dis-* in front of *-ambiguation* means that a word may be ambiguous; that it can have more than one meaning, and that we have to address and resolve the possible confusion. In short, *disambiguation* in *Wikipedia* means that an editor has recognized that more than one possible meaning exists, and has separated one from the other. Humans make this distinction and separation without difficulty. A computer needs context in order to do this.

The next chapter in this book is dedicated to textual disambiguation. For that reason, we will give only a very cursory description here.

From a high level perspective, Textual ETL is technology that ingests text and turns that text into a database, complete with context.

Textual ETL—Ingesting Text

Figure 10.7 depicts the high level functionality of Textual ETL. It shows that the text is being gathered and processed through several levels (or iterations). The result is a database. Once the database is produced, the database can be both archived and analyzed; then it can be visualized. It is the visualization that end users find to be so insightful.[6] While the technology depicted in Figure 10.7 is interesting in its own right (and will be discussed in depth), a separate discussion is in order here.

One of the real values in reading text and passing text through a process such as Textual ETL is ultimately in the ability to process huge amounts of it. Take any collection of text, such as medical records,

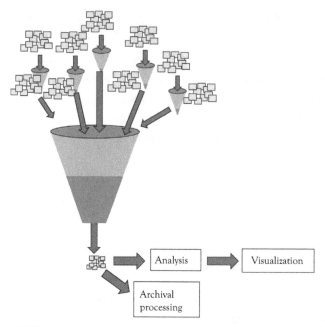

Figure 10.7

customer or employee complaints, contracts, or warranties, and attempt to read and digest the text manually. In most contexts, any attempt to read and digest any substantial amount of text manually has its limitations. Tolstoy's *War and Peace* is an exhausting 1,225 pages,[7] but imagine reading a thousand books of that length (over 1.2 million pages) or 10,000 warranty claims.

The act of reading is time consuming and the amount of data that can be mentally remembered is finite. Once the volume of the text starts to exceed the mental capacity of the reader, there is no point in trying to read and digest more information.

But placing the text inside a computer gives a user for all practical purposes the ability to read a nearly infinite amount of material. A computer can read and digest many orders of magnitude, more information than can individual any. Therefore, when it comes to large volumes of text, computer storage is far more effective and efficient at the task than any human attempt to capture and digest the same information.

So will we learn to speak *computer*? No. None of us will learn to speak *binary*. Machine language is for machines.

Output of Textual ETL

The output of Textual ETL is a database. Once text is put into the form of a database it can handle millions and millions of records.

But there is a problem with a database. The problem is that data in a database is not useful for decision-making purposes until the data can be visualized. Stated differently, it is very difficult to use raw data in a database for the purpose of making decisions. But it is easy to use that same data for the purpose of making decisions when the data can be visualized. Figure 10.8 is a reminder that raw data is unfit for the purpose of making decisions, but that visualized data is designed for that purpose.

Sources of Data

The data that flows into the Big Data environment comes from a wide variety of sources.

Figure 10.9 shows some of those typical sources.

One source of data flowing into Big Data is tape. Magnetic tape is still widely used for many purposes: archival processing, as a store for analog processing, as a collection point for network processing, and so forth. In many cases, the inexpensiveness and versatility of magnetic tape make it popular as a medium to collect and store data.

Easily the most ubiquitous source of data for Big Data is standard magnetic disk storage. Disk storage is found in many places. We're familiar with being on a mainframe environment, the personal computer

Aaland, Joan 00191 Jun 25, 2014 appendectomy...
Allred, Gene 00298 Jul 20, 2015 tonsilectomy...
Aanonsen, Gary Jul 13, 2104 exploratory surgery....
Brown, Robert Aug 2, 2013 knee replacement.....
Borels, Mary Sept 30, 2013 histerectomy.....
Carrasco, Joe Oct 12, 2011 kidney removal....
Cialone, Joe Nov 18, 2014 kidney stones.....
Chiavarro, Maria Dec 2, 2013 gall bladder.....
Dion, Cialane Jan 2015 appendectomy.....
Folmer, Jonathon Feb 18, 2015 heart transplant....
Brewer, Dink Mar 13, 2012 liver replacement....
Combs, James Apr 12, 2013 kidney transplant.....
Sutherlin, Mike May 30, 2012 hand surgery.....
Corbin, Ken June 23, 2014 blood transfusion.....

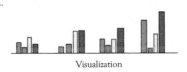

Visualization

Database

Figure 10.8

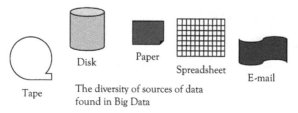

Tape

Disk

Paper

Spreadsheet

E-mail

The diversity of sources of data found in Big Data

Figure 10.9

environment, as a portable hard drive connected to a work station, and so forth. Disk storage is versatile and widely used.

Another storage medium for Big Data is the paper environment. Contracts, news articles, memoranda, letters, negotiations, and so on, all find their way onto paper. Paper is easily read by practically anyone and is historically a widely used medium. In the context of litigation in days gone by, when one party wanted potentially relevant documents in a dispute from the opposing party, and both sides were asked to produce such documents, all anyone had to do was open up a file drawer and pull out the files. Those days are gone.

Another widely used medium is that of the spreadsheet. Spreadsheets are used in business for many purposes. Spreadsheets are popular for many reasons: versatility, their ability to manage data, the immediate availability, and so forth. But perhaps their biggest reason for widespread usage is that end users can use spreadsheets in different ways: for example, as mini data bases, for *what if* constructs, and for reports and presentations using tables and graphs.

Another widespread medium for nonrepetitive data is that of e-mails. E-mails are now used as a communication medium all across the world, and they are found in, if not central to, every business.

All of these communication media hold nonrepetitive data that are candidates for being stored in Big Data.

Optical Character Recognition

One medium in particular still holds a special interest for us, and that medium is paper. Paper has been the medium by which communications have been conducted since the days of Guttenberg and the printing press.

Not only is print found everywhere, print has been used for a long, long time. It is the medium for recording one person's thoughts (and intentions) and engaging in telepathy with his or her readers, whether known or unknown.

In order to turn print into an electronically recognizable format, it is necessary to pass print through technology called *optical character recognition* (OCR). Figure 10.10 depicts OCR technology and the process of converting print into electronically recognizable text.

All of the different media need some sort of transformation technology in order to have their content placed into Big Data. Big Data is of course a digital world. And while some say that *content* in a digital environment is King, the Emperor would have no clothes without a transforming intermediary. Figure 10.11 shows that in one way or the other, data is transported from the originating medium into Big Data.

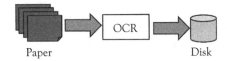

Figure 10.10

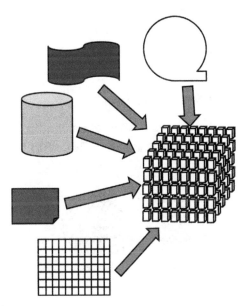

Figure 10.11

In some cases, the transformation is done in a very simple manner, by means of a simple load technology. In other cases, the transformation is made by very sophisticated technology such as passing text through Textual ETL.

Big Data and Litigation

So why is Big Data an enabling technology for a system to prevent litigation? Big Data has the following necessary properties:

- Big Data is capable of holding an almost unlimited amount of data.
- Big Data is capable of holding nonrepetitive data that has been contextualized.
- Big Data is capable of holding data at a very reasonable cost.

Figure 10.12 shows that there is a significant cost differential between classical disk storage and Big Data.

Simply stated, Big Data holds data at a fraction of the cost of classical high performance disk storage. For all of these reasons then, Big Data is one of the enabling factors for a proactive system to provide *early warning* of potential litigation. The early proponents of preventive law had no access to this technology.

The Infrastructure Surrounding Big Data

It is worthwhile noting that, for a variety of reasons, Big Data normally is surrounded by an infrastructure, as seen in Figure 10.13.

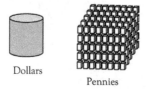

Dollars

Pennies

Figure 10.12

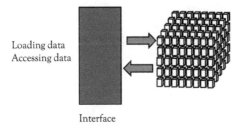

Loading data
Accessing data

Interface

Figure 10.13

There are a lot of different kinds of functional needs for an infra-structure that surrounds Big Data. The two most basic of these functions are (1) loading data into Big Data and (2) accessing that data once it is loaded. We turn now to this subject.

CHAPTER 11

Textual Disambiguation— Integrating Text into a Database

When looking for the early warning signs of a lawsuit, an analyst soon discovers that there are many documents (and many types of documents) to read and analyze. It is tempting to suggest that one or more persons should just sit down and read the documents that are likely to contain early warning information. However, anyone attempting to implement this suggestion would quickly discover that the process of manually reading and analyzing documents has its own severe drawbacks. Figure 11.1 shows the manual processing of documents.

The two impediments to manually processing documents are the time that it takes to read the documents and the limited capacity of a human brain to remember the contents of each of them. There is a very finite capacity for reading and remembering the contents of a document in the human brain or even a team of brilliant readers.

The amount of documents that must be processed, and the speed with which the documents must be processed, is such that manual processing of documents for the purpose of detecting the risk of potential litigation is simply not a possibility.

Automation of Document Processing

In order to create a credible approach to processing documents, eDiscovery practitioners, years ago, reached the conclusion that automation of the processing of the contents of the text in the documents was the only practical approach. Once the text in the document is read and analyzed in an automated manner, the volume of documents that can be processed and the speed with which the processing can be done, increases by many orders of magnitude. Figure 11.2 shows that automation must be used in order to process the documents that are needed to *see* potential litigation before there is any damage.

The first step is the automation of the capturing of text from the document. Herein lies the first major challenge for automating the system. The fundamental challenge in the automation of the processing of a document is that databases require a neatly defined, well-structured organization of data. One of the secrets of computer processing is that much of the speed and efficiency of computer automated processing relies on the fact that data is organized this way. Figure 11.3 shows that databases and computers require that data be organized in a highly structured manner.

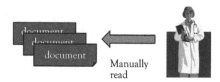

Manually
read

Figure 11.1

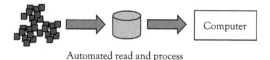

Automated read and process

Figure 11.2

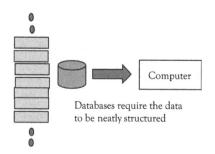

Databases require the data
to be neatly structured

Figure 11.3

The Disorganization of Raw Text

But when one looks at raw text, a simple truth emerges: Raw text is anything but organized and orderly. Figure 11.4 depicts the point that raw text has a hard time fitting into the rigid format and structure required by the computer.

In actuality, raw text has a *really hard time*!

This problem led me to create a software called Textual ETL. One of the primary purposes of Textual ETL is to read electronically based *unstructured* text, and to then do the things that are needed in order to place that unstructured text into the form and structure needed by a computer. Figure 11.5 shows that one of the most basic functions of Textual ETL is to create a structure for unstructured text:

There are many functions that need to be done in order to achieve this structuring of text. Some of the functions include but are not limited to:

- Editing and correcting spelling;
- Removal of stop words (for example, too common words such as *a* and *the*);
- Creation of word stems (such as *edit* instead of *editing* or *editorial*);
- Resolution of acronyms;
- Negation resolution—both simple and complex; and
- Proximity variable resolution (meaning a word within a specified distance from another word).

When Textual ETL finishes doing its job of processing, the formerly unstructured raw text is able to be placed into an organized standard database. Figure 11.6 depicts some of the functions required to restructure text into an organized format.

Context

But restructuring text is only one of the major functions of Textual ETL. Another, and more important, function of Textual ETL is to derive and identify the *context* of certain words in the raw text. There are many ways

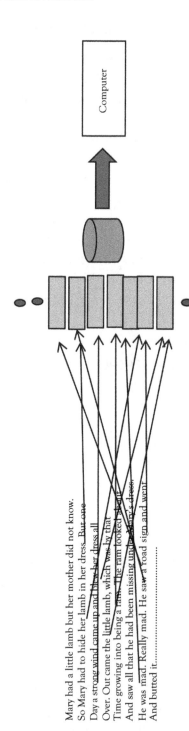

Figure 11.4

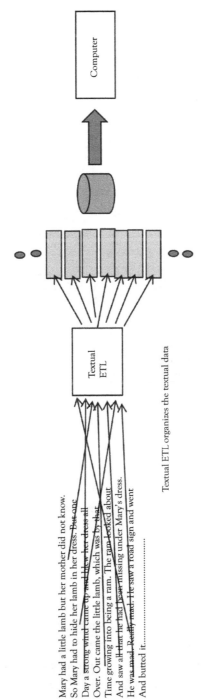

Textual ETL organizes the textual data

Figure 11.5

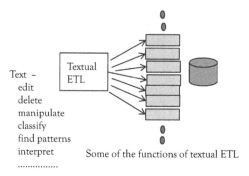

Some of the functions of textual ETL

Figure 11.6

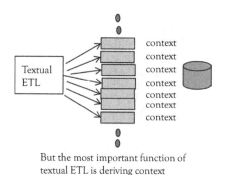

But the most important function of
textual ETL is deriving context

Figure 11.7

that context is derived. Figure 11.7 emphasizes that Textual ETL derives context from textual input.

Because of the complexity of language, there is no one single way to derive context. Instead there are many ways to derive context. And in some cases, more than one technique for the derivation of context is needed, even for the same word.

Deriving Context

Most of context is external to text (as has been previously discussed). Therefore it should not come as a surprise that much of the process of contextualization of text depends on externally applied factors. Some of the many techniques of contextualization include but are not limited to the following:

- Taxonomy resolution, where an external taxonomy or taxonomies are used to clarify or classify words found in raw text;
- Inline contextualization, where predictable text can be used to identify and classify words and phrases found in raw text;
- Custom variables, where the mere pattern of a variable can be used to classify a word or phrase;
- Proximity variables, where the proximity of two or more words or classifications can be used to classify a concept or entity;
- Homographic resolution, where identifying the background of an author of a document can provide the basis for the proper classification of a word or phrase;
- Stop word processing, where the removal of certain words from the raw text of a document can be considered to be a form of classification; and
- Acronym resolution, where the resolution of acronyms is a rough form of contextualization.

Figure 11.8 shows some of the more important forms of contextualization.

Taxonomy Resolution

While there are many different ways that contextualization can occur, perhaps the most significant way contextualization occurs is through taxonomy resolution. As a simple example of taxonomy resolution, suppose that we have a taxonomy as shown in Figure 11.9.

In this simple taxonomy, we see that a car can be a Porsche, Ford, Honda, Volkswagen, or a Ferrari. If the industry in which Textual ETL involves automobiles (such as automotive repair), Textual ETL would be configured to use this taxonomy. Then, when raw text is read, Textual ETL makes a comparison to see if a word from the raw text is found in that taxonomy or one of the other applicable taxonomies: sentiment taxonomies and subject matter (*hot word*) taxonomies.

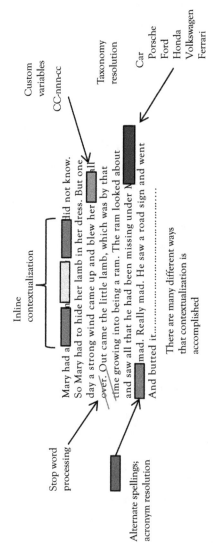

Figure 11.8

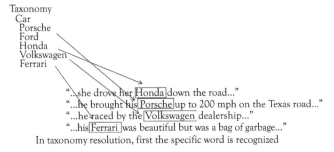

In taxonomy resolution, first the specific word is recognized

Figure 11.9

"...she drove her Honda /car down the road..."
"...he brought his Porsche /car up to 200 mph on the Texas road..."
"...he raced by the Volkswagen /car dealership..."
"...his Ferrari /car was beautiful but was a bag of garbage..."

After the specific word is recognized, the generic classification is added

Figure 11.10

Upon reading the raw text and finding the word in one of the taxonomies, the software finds that a Honda is a car, a Porsche is a car, a Volkswagen is a car, and a Ferrari is a car.

Once the raw text is read, the raw text is appended with the recognition of what the taxonomy has been determined to be. Figure 11.10 shows how Textual ETL appends the taxonomy classification to the raw text.

We should pause to make a couple of observations here. The first observation is that the simple example shown in the preceding figure masks a whole level of complexity. In reality, taxonomy resolution is much more complex than the simple case we have used in this illustration. To avoid going off on this tangent, we won't say more.

A second observation is that upon having done taxonomy resolution, an analyst looking at the data can now do queries that are simply not possible without having done taxonomy processing. For example, look at the data shown in Figure 11.10. Now an analyst can pose a query to find all cars. Because of our taxonomy example, Textual ETL can locate each instance where the creator of the unstructured text referred to a car, regardless of whether the author was referring to Hondas, Porsches, Volkswagens, or Ferraris.

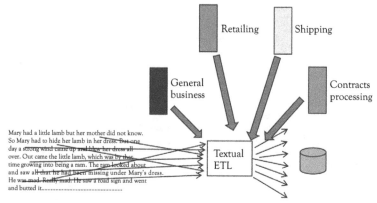

Different taxonomies are used for different

Figure 11.11

A third observation is that taxonomies are an external means of identifying context. Depending on how Textual ETL is configured, an analyst can choose from one or many taxonomies that apply. The analyst, upon preparing to do Textual ETL processing, chooses which taxonomies to use. The taxonomies are typically chosen from the libraries of a provider, such as WAND Inc., the world's largest purveyor of pre-prepared taxonomies.

For example, in Figure 11.11, we indicate that the analyst has chosen to use taxonomies that are relevant to the business of the organization. In Figure 11.11, the products and services taxonomies are General business, Retailing, and Shipping.

In Figure 11.11, our hypothetical analyst has chosen to use taxonomies that would apply to a general purpose retailing and shipping organization. Note that the taxonomies may be added together. If the organization had been a manufacturer, a completely different set of taxonomies would have been chosen. The selection of taxonomies depends entirely on the business or industry sector of interest, and even on the type of data within the business, as seen in Figure 11.12.

Mapping

Different document types require different definitions. Contextualization and restructuring algorithms are called the *mapping* of a document. Each

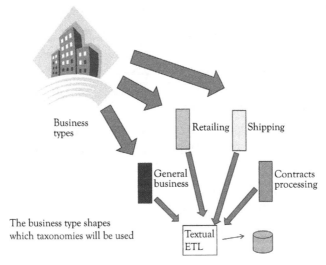

Figure 11.12

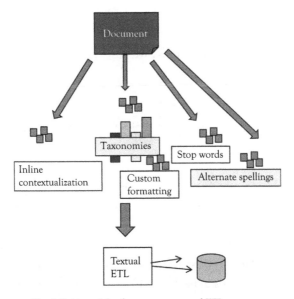

The definition of the document to textual ETL
is called *mapping*.

Figure 11.13

document type will have its own unique mapping. Figure 11.13 shows
the mapping that has been created for a document type.

We are beginning to see that the amount of configuring that goes into Textual ETL is not trivial. Indeed, there is no question that the most intellectually challenging aspect of using Textual ETL is that of mapping. From both a complexity perspective and from a completeness standpoint, mapping represents a significant investment for the organization that engages in Textual ETL processing.

Once the mapping is done properly and completely, it directs the system and Textual ETL as to how a given type of document should be processed.

But suppose an organization does mapping for one week and processes the documents specified by the mapping. Then suppose that, during the next week, the organization does some more mappings. Then, during the third week, the organization needs to go back and reprocess some more of the document types that were processed in the first week.

Does the organization have to recreate the mappings that were created in the first week? The answer is no.

The Move-Remove Facility

At the end of the mapping process, the organization stores the mappings that have been created in a facility called the *Move-Remove* facility. For this reason, and in the context of our early warning system, the taxonomy mappings for the subjects of *product liability* and the different types of workplace discrimination are stored, but are not static.

In the Move-Remove facility, each mapping is stored, along with an identifier that allows the analyst to identify it. Then, at a later point in time, the organization can simply return to the Move-Remove facility, restore the mapping that is desired, and commence to process against the document type. For this reason, it is not necessary to recreate a mapping if more processing needs to be done with respect to a document type that has already been defined.

Figure 11.14 indicates the Move-Remove facility.

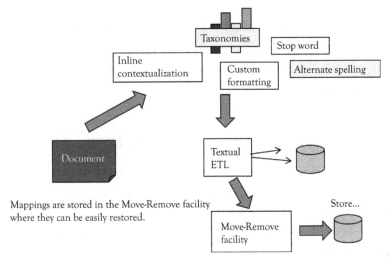

Figure 11.14

Post-processing

Another feature of Textual ETL is the *post process* module. The post-process module is used to restructure the output of standard Textual ETL processing. The output of standard ETL processing is data that can be called *normalized text.*

The normalized text is quite simple data, but has many implications. There are considerations of the order in which words appear, the placement of periods, the occurrence of negations, and so forth. In truth, the normalized text is deceptive in that the many implications found there are not obvious to the untrained eye.

To that end, in some cases, it is useful to take the normalized text, which is the output of Textual ETL, and restructure it so that it is easy to use and intuitive to understand. Documents such as contracts, memoranda, medical records, and so forth are all restructured. The restructuring is done in the postprocess module, as depicted in Figure 11.15.

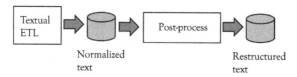

Figure 11.15

Restructured Text Goes into a Database

When all is said and done, Textual ETL is the software technology that allows unstructured text to be placed inside a database. Once the text is placed inside the database, an unlimited number of documents can be processed, and the time required for processing those documents is not unreasonable. In fact, we have processed over 600,000 e-mails in minutes and found responsive documents in only a few seconds.

Figure 11.16 shows the architectural rendition of Textual ETL.

Now to this transformational idea of a litigation early warning system, we have added a breakthrough technology, Textual ETL. Textual ETL opens the gateway to actually being able to prevent litigation. Without the advent of Big Data and an invention like Textual ETL, any effort to achieve this result, either manually or anecdotally, would amount to nothing more than wishful thinking.

We've been slowly describing Textual ETL, step-by-step, but we haven't visualized any data yet. That's next.

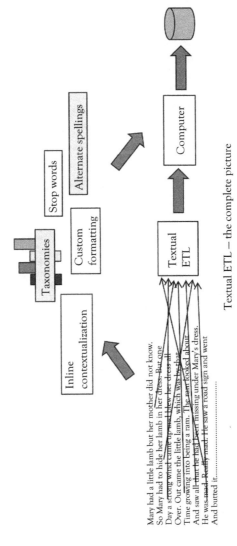

Textual ETL – the complete picture

Figure 11.16

CHAPTER 12

Visualization

The ability to take unstructured text and transform it into a database format, and then derive context from it, is a large achievement unto itself. But there is a problem with the output of Textual ETL. Figure 12.1 illustrates a simplified architectural rendition of Textual ETL.

The problem with the output from Textual ETL is that visualization is difficult. Unless a person is looking for a single specific word, which is almost never the case, the output directly from Textual ETL is difficult to use.

Patterns

What most people are looking for from the output of Textual ETL is patterns. And patterns are formed by multiple occurrences of data, where the instances of data are gathered, organized, and accumulated. Figure 12.2 shows some typical output from Textual ETL.

From the direct output shown in Figure 12.2, it is easy to see why it is difficult to make sense of Textual ETL. Data appears in one occurrence after another in a flat file. Trying to find meaning in such a file is difficult to do. Figure 12.3 illustrates that the direct output from Textual ETL can be bewildering.

Because the output directly obtained from Textual ETL is difficult to use for analytical purposes, it is almost always a good idea to take the output from Textual ETL and to pass it through analytical software, as seen in Figure 12.4.

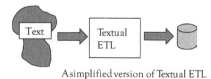

A simplified version of Textual ETL

Figure 12.1

The output database

Figure 12.2

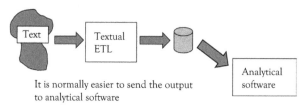

Figure 12.3

It is normally easier to send the output
to analytical software

Figure 12.4

Analytics Software

Analytical software is capable of taking the output from Textual ETL and manipulating the data. The analytical software can do such things as:

- Group data into classifications and subclassifications;
- Summarize data together; and
- Compare and contrast data.

Analytical software is capable of organizing and preparing the output from Textual ETL and presenting the output in a form that is useful and meaningful to the end user. The results of Textual ETL are much more easily understood by looking at the data after it has been passed through analytical software, as seen in Figure 12.5.

There are many reasons why visualizations are much more meaningful than raw data. The primary reason is that when visualized properly, patterns stick out and are very obvious. And it is not just one pattern that can be identified; multiple patterns become obvious.

It is up to the analyst to do (at least) two things: (1) create visualizations that make the patterns obvious and (2) be alert to which patterns might be occurring in the data.

To bring this point back to our litigation early warning system, Textual ETL might report out an e-mail as a potential threat of a certain type of litigation. In that case, the pattern would be seen in the words of the e-mail. Are there sentiment words or phrases within close proximity to words or phrases pertaining to the *hot words* of a particular subject matter? If Textual ETL were ingesting warranty claims, for example, the pattern might be seen in the frequency of certain problems in the claims. How many claims pertained to the same topic or key word, such as *ignition*?

Some Common Forms of Visualization

Using analytical software, an analyst has a wide variety of ways to visualize data. Figure 12.6 shows some of the common ways that data can be visualized.

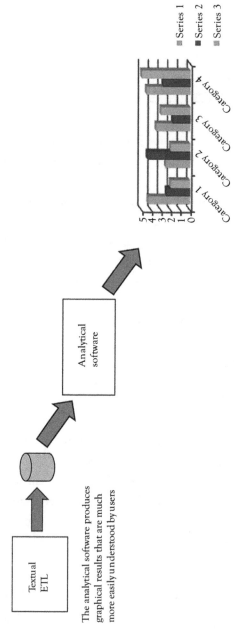

The analytical software produces graphical results that are much more easily understood by users

Figure 12.5

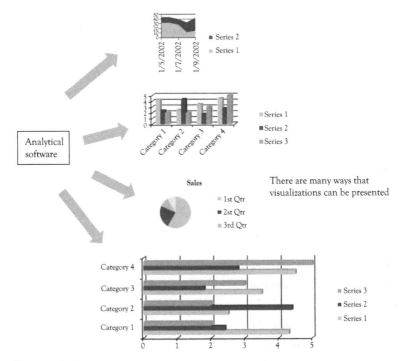

Figure 12.6

In other words, data can be visualized as a continuous comparison of multiple variables over time. Or data can be depicted as a Pareto chart of multiple variables measured over time. Another way to visualize data is as a pie chart.

In the case of textual data, the number of times the data occurs or a comparison of the data classification are common ways to visualize data for the purpose of finding patterns.

Statistical Analysis

Visualizations serve the purpose of displaying information. But occasionally it is useful to do statistical analysis on data. Figure 12.7 shows that, in addition to the display of data, statistical analysis can be done on data that has been placed into the form and structure of a database, and where the data has been contextualized.

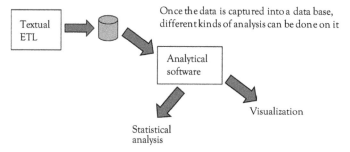

Textual ETL

Once the data is captured into a data base, different kinds of analysis can be done on it

Analytical software

Visualization

Statistical analysis

Figure 12.7

Measuring Data Over Time

Data can be examined in several ways. One way to examine data is over time. When data is examined over time, a variable is measured over a unit of time, such as the end of the month, or the end of the year. Figure 12.8 shows the measurement of data over time.

While data that is measured over time is interesting, sometimes it is useful to measure different variables over the same unit of time. Figure 12.9 shows the measurement of multiple variables over time.

Yet another approach to the display of variables is the correlative display of points of data. Different points of data are placed on a graph and a regression analysis is performed, which is sometimes called the *least squares* method. Data-fitting produces a relationship (a function) that displays the best fit of the function to the data. Figure 12.10 depicts this visualization of data.

Separating Data by Classifications

Throughout the whole process of visualization, it is almost always useful to separate data into different classifications.[1] When data is not separated by classes, the patterns relating to the data become very difficult to see.

One way to determine patterns is to look at
data across time

Figure 12.8

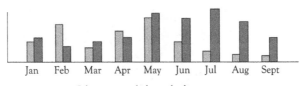

Often times it helps to look at more
than one variable across time

Figure 12.9

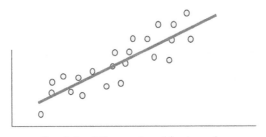

Correlating different points of data is another
good way to determine patterns

Figure 12.10

Therefore, a basic and important first step in finding patterns is to separate data out by classifications. Figure 12.11 shows the separation of data
into different classifications.

Once the data has been separated into different classes, it can then be summarized, examined over time, and further analyzed to look for patterns. Figure 12.12 shows the summarization of data after it has been classified.

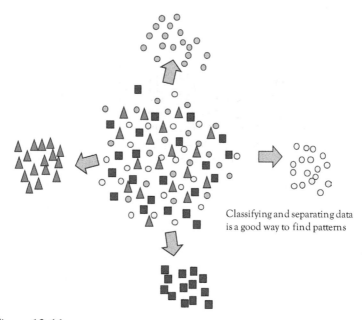

Classifying and separating data
is a good way to find patterns

Figure 12.11

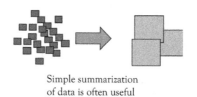

Simple summarization
of data is often useful

Figure 12.12

CHAPTER 13

Two Examples of Document Types

While descriptions of technology and architectural renditions are interesting and useful in their own ways, some actual examples provide another perspective. In this chapter, two different types of documents will be described. The first type relates to e-mails and other forms of internal communications. The second example relates to corporate call center activity, where the source of unstructured text is external.[1]

In the first case, the organization may be looking for potential discrimination activities, where one employee sends an e-mail to another employee. In the second example, warranty claims are examined. By looking at warranty claims, the organization may be alerted to a potential product liability lawsuit.

There are some similarities in the examples. But there are many important differences as well.

Examining E-mails

The hunt for a potential discrimination lawsuit focuses on e-mails. And that e-mail is behind the firewall. In other words, our focus is *internal* e-mails, from employee to employee. It is possible that other types of e-mails may be relevant, but far and away; the e-mails that are likely to hold the information potentially relevant to a possible discrimination lawsuit are internally generated e-mails. They betray intention. Where there is e-smoke, there is, potentially, a future e-fire. Figure 13.1 is a reminder that e-mails are the center of attention when an organization is looking for potential workplace discrimination complaints.

It is worth noting that the kinds of discrimination we would like to spot, before the damage is done, are all kinds of illegal discriminatory

E-mail

Figure 13.1

intentions expressed in words; that is, discrimination based on race, gender, age, and so on. This is a relatively limited set. We provided the list earlier in the book, but so that you don't have to hunt for it, the categories of discriminatory misbehavior are:

- Age
- Disability
- Equal pay or compensation
- Genetic information
- Harassment
- National origin
- Pregnancy
- Race or color
- Religion
- Retaliation
- Sex
- Sexual harassment

As might be expected, people use certain words in the course of violating each one of these categories. There may be overlap, especially in the case of retaliation, but in general the taxonomy for age discrimination is different from the taxonomy for racial discrimination or sexual harassment.

But when working with e-mails, there are many challenges. The first challenge is that of dealing with the sheer volume of e-mails. A large corporation may have millions of e-mails generated daily, and each e-mail has to be examined.

The Volume of E-mails

Figure 13.2 shows that the first challenge in examining e-mails is the challenge of dealing with the volume of e-mails that are generated.

The first challenge of e-mails —
the volume

Figure 13.2

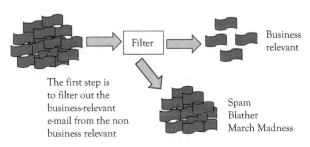

Figure 13.3

The first step in examining the e-mails is to eliminate the irrelevant e-mails. We do this by means of yet another taxonomy, which acts like a filter. The e-mails are passed through the filter, and all of the e-mails that are not directly related to the business of the corporation are eliminated. Figure 13.3 shows the elimination of nonrelevant e-mails, which leaves us with only the business-relevant e-mails.

Generally speaking, there are three types of e-mails found in an e-mail stream: business-relevant e-mail, spam, and blather. Spam is e-mail that is not business relevant and that has been generated from a source external to the corporation. Blather is e-mail generated internal to the corporation that is not business relevant. A simple example of blather is the sharing of a joke that is passed throughout the office. Another example is the sharing of sports topics, such as March Madness brackets.

In addition to filtering out spam and blather, the filter also removes a lot of system information that is needed by the system for the operation of the e-mail environment, but which has nothing to do with the messages that are being passed through the system. The net result of the filter is the reduction of the e-mail stream to a more workable, manageable volume of data. Figure 13.4 illustrates the filter process.

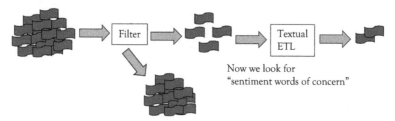

Now we look for
"sentiment words of concern"

Figure 13.4

Passing E-mail Through Textual ETL

After the e-mails have been filtered, the next step is to read the e-mails and pass the data through Textual ETL. The data is passed through Textual ETL and it looks for words that might indicate that there is some dissension based on a type of discrimination. There are two components to such dissension: (1) sentiment words and (2) subject matter words.

In one of the 2014 exemplary cases we discussed previously, the Complaint quoted the defendant as saying, "I hate pregnant women." Here we have one sentiment word *hate* combined with potentially two forms of discrimination: gender discrimination and discrimination based on a medical condition (pregnancy).

As a general rule, several iterations of the processing are made. This iterative processing is typically the case at the beginning of the analytical process. The need for iterative processing is caused by several factors:

- The complexity of documents;
- The fact that the end user does not know what he or she wants at the outset; and
- The optional capabilities built into Textual ETL.

For these reasons and more, it is normal for an analyst who is creating the taxonomies to configure Textual ETL to perform many iterations of analysis against a prechosen set of documents, especially as the analyst first encounters a new document type. Figure 13.5 shows that iterative processing of a document type is the norm.

After an analyst feels comfortable that he or she can process against the documents, the analyst then embarks on a serious analysis of the

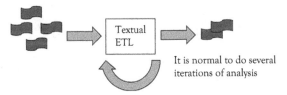

It is normal to do several
iterations of analysis

Figure 13.5

documents for the purpose of finding potential discrimination lawsuits. To this end, the analyst uses what are called the *words of concern*. In a nutshell, the words of concern are the list of words that are indicative of a person being upset, perhaps because a product appears to be dangerous or because of some form of discrimination.

Just as a particular business taxonomy was used to qualify e-mails for business relevancy, now a sentiment taxonomy, the *words of concern*, forms the basis for the second *paring down* of e-mails.

Further Analysis

After the *words of concern* are used for analysis, the next step is to further pare down the e-mails. This third paring is done on the basis of one or more criteria:

- Looking for *hot words*. Hot words are words of concern that by themselves cause alarms to go off.
- Looking for words in combination or proximity to each other. In proximity analysis, the objective is to find word groups used in conjunction with each other. Textual ETL is able to find *proximity words* within a user variable called *byte separation*.
- Sorting words by number of occurrences. After all the analysis is done, it may be useful to sort the qualifying e-mails by the number of occurrences. Some e-mails will have only one word of concern (or hot word) whereas other e-mails may have multiple words of concern or hot words.

Figure 13.6 shows this third level of qualification of e-mails:

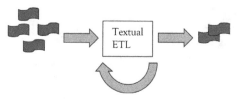

After words of concern are established—
we look for subject matter *hot words*
proximity words sorted sequences of words
analysis is done, in an iterative manner

Figure 13.6

After the three levels of qualification, the organization is left with a finite number of e-mails. But there may be false positives.

So now an *attorney* analyst needs to look at the output. It is now up to the legal department to determine if the qualifying e-mails present a threat or not.

Analysis by the Legal Department

Figure 13.7 shows that a legal department needs to examine the qualifying e-mails to see if the e-mails represent a concern to the organization and whether management has been sufficiently enabled to be proactive.

The net effect of the process that we have described is to take the task of examining the e-mails the enterprise has generated, for example, the previous day, and reduce the task to a workable, manageable one. It is theoretically possible for a lawyer or manager to read all the e-mails that pass through the organization. But this is only theoretically possible. No organization has the time and resources to manually read every e-mail created within the organization.

Instead, the organization enlists the computer and Textual ETL to filter out the e-mails that don't represent a litigation risk to the organization. Then, after the troublesome e-mails are identified, in-house counsel can sit down and read the e-mails that represent a threat.

In the past, no such tool has existed. Figure 13.8 depicts those e-mails that have been filtered, such that reading the filtered e-mails is a task that can be accomplished in a finite amount of time.

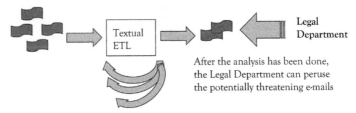

After the analysis has been done, the Legal Department can peruse the potentially threatening e-mails

Figure 13.7

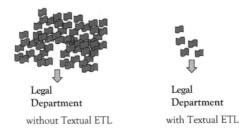

Legal
Department
without Textual ETL

Legal
Department
with Textual ETL

Figure 13.8

Product Liability Analysis

Another type of early warning is that of anticipating a product liability lawsuit. There are actually many places to look for product liability lawsuits. Besides e-mails, two of the most likely places are corporate call center conversations and warranty claim data.

The discussion in this chapter focuses on warranty claim data. However, we note that warranty claims are hardly the only place to look for potential product liability cases. Figure 13.9 indicates a product warranty.

The place to start to process warranty data is to examine the warranty. Typically we start by creating taxonomies. The taxonomies focus on such things as:

- Product features
- Product guarantees
- Implied product lifetime
- Product usage
- Product capacity
- Product installation procedures

A warranty

Figure 13.9

Mapping the Warranty

Figure 13.10 illustrates the mapping that is done for a warranty.

After the mapping is done (or at least the first iteration of the mapping is done), the next step is to run Textual ETL. In fact Textual ETL is run iteratively because it is highly likely that the first iteration of mapping will not be correct. Figure 13.11 shows the iterative processing that occurs.

After the database is created and the analyst is satisfied that the data is correct and complete, the next step is to create visualizations from the database. Figure 13.12 shows the analysis that is created from the database.

The analysis can be created in many ways with many forms of visualization. And there are many things the analyst can choose to visualize. However, typically the things the analyst chooses to look at include:

- The number of recurring warranties;
- The potential seriousness of the warranty; and
- Any new types of warranty patterns that are emerging.

Visualizing the Results

Figure 13.13 shows types of things an analyst would probably choose to visualize:

Of course, the results found in the database are kept over time. Being able to compare visualizations over time is a useful tool as well. And

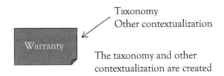

Figure 13.10

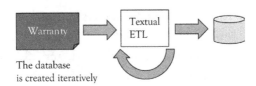

Figure 13.11

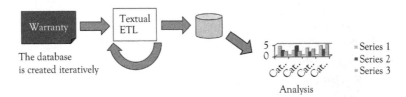

Figure 13.12

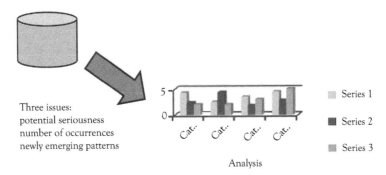

Figure 13.13

warranties are not the only place to look. Some of the other likely places to look include.

- E-mails
- Call center transcriptions
- Tweets

Figure 13.14 depicts possible other sources for anticipatory analysis of product liability lawsuits.

While the discussion has focusedw on warranty claims, the same processing path could have been used for any of the other source of data and any other type of lawsuit.

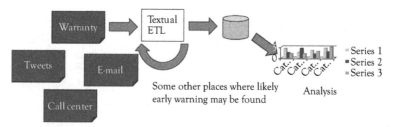

Some other places where likely early warning may be found

Analysis

Figure 13.14

CHAPTER 14

Summary: Textual ETL from an Architectural Perspective

The discussions beginning with Chapter 10 have been at a more technical level, to better explain Textual ETL and how an early warning system would work. There is nothing wrong with those discussions and they are necessary. However, to provide a better perspective, let's stand back and look at the larger picture.

This chapter is a higher level architectural perspective of the dynamics of what is required to implement this system.

Filtering Data

From a higher perspective, when you look at ingesting text and then reading and processing it, the process amounts to a large filtering process.

There is a lot of textual data to be digested, so much so that processing it manually is not a viable alternative. In addition, text is very uneven. For example, text comes in many forms: slang, formal language, text messaging, acronyms, and so on. Text also comes in many languages: English, Spanish, Mandarin, Portuguese, Russian, and so on. Within a given language there are many loose ends: double meanings, obscure meanings, highly specialized meanings such as those found in medical technology, colloquialisms, and so forth.

Then there is the structure of text: paragraphs, sentences, spelling, formal documents, transcripts of casual conversation, and so on.

In short, language is inherently complex.

Our first job is to cope with the volume of text that is present. To this end, as Figure 14.1 illustrates, text is passed through a series of *siphons* or *filters* by the technology of Textual ETL as it is applied to this particular use case.

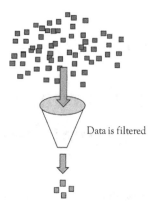

Data is filtered

Figure 14.1

There are many techniques that are used in Textual ETL for handling volume. Textual ETL typically employs more than one technique at a time.

Parallel Processing

One technique employed by Textual ETL to cope with the high volumes of data the system must evaluate is that of operating different processes in parallel. Figure 14.2 shows that Textual ETL is capable of processing text on different computers at the same time.

By running on separate machines at the same time, the elapsed time required to process the workload can be cut significantly. If m units of time are required to process a workload, then the elapsed can be cut by n units where n is the number of processors that can be employed. Stated differently, if m units of time are required to process a workload, then m/n units of time are required to process the workload when the workload is divided over n different processors.

Processing in parallel has the potential for greatly reducing the elapsed amount of time required to run a large amount of data.

Big Data Technology

Another technique that can be employed by Textual ETL to manage the volume of data that the system must encounter is to take advantage of Big Data technology. Figure 14.3 depicts the usage of Big Data technology.

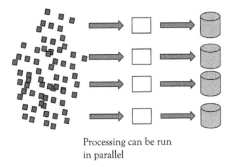

Processing can be run
in parallel

Figure 14.2

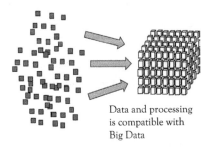

Data and processing
is compatible with
Big Data

Figure 14.3

There are many advantages to using Big Data technology such as Hadoop.[1] The following are some of the advantages:

- Big Data is less expensive than other forms of storage.
- Big Data is equipped to handle very large volumes of data.
- Big Data is architecturally geared for handling data in a parallel manner.

Large Processors

A third approach to handling large amounts of data is to use a large processor. Figure 14.4 depicts the usage of a large processor to read and process large amounts of text.

The problem with using a large processor for handling large amounts of text is that the larger the processor, the more expensive the processing becomes. In addition, there is always an upper end of data that can be

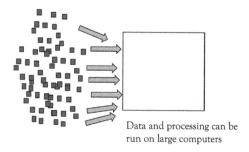

Data and processing can be
run on large computers

Figure 14.4

processed by a large processor. Once the analyst surpasses the upper end of the capacity of the large processor, the analyst is forced into adopting another strategy.

These then are three of the approaches that can be taken to allow the analyst to cope with the large volumes of data that will be encountered in the processing of text.

But volumes of data are not the only challenge. A second challenge of processing is dealing with text itself. Some processing systems just don't deal with text at all. Other processing systems deal with text, but at a very superficial level.

Dealing with Text

However Textual ETL is specifically designed to deal with text. Figure 14.5 depicts Textual ETL.

Textual ETL not only reads and manages text, it does so at a very profound level. Textual ETL reads and manages text at the *contextual* level. Figure 14.6 indicates that Textual ETL operates at the contextual level.

The real challenge of operating at the contextual level is the fact that most context of text is external to the text itself. If all you look at is text, there is very little you know about the context of the text. Textual ETL knows this and is equipped to operate at the external level as well as at the internal level.

There are many ways that Textual ETL operates at the external level. The primary way (but hardly the only way) that Textual ETL operates at

Read and manage text

Figure 14.5

The ability to handle both text and context

Figure 14.6

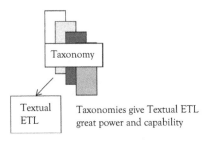

Figure 14.7

the external level is through the integration of taxonomies with the processed text, as shown in Figure 14.7.

Taxonomies

External taxonomies provide great range for the text being processed by Textual ETL. While there are an almost infinite number of possibilities for taxonomies, there exist a very large collection of taxonomies that are available through third party vendors, such as WAND Inc. It is easy enough to find and use one or more of the many taxonomies supplied by WAND.[2]

But even though WAND's taxonomies are readily available, they still need some amount of customization upon usage. Even with customization, it is a quick and easy thing to simply apply the taxonomies to Textual ETL. And in doing so the perspective of external context is readily applied to the text that needs to be processed.

Different Languages

Another important aspect of using Textual ETL is that Textual ETL is not limited to the English language. Figure 14.8 shows that Textual ETL operates in many languages found throughout the world.

Textual ETL also operates on any kind of language. Figure 14.9 shows that Textual ETL operates on formal language, slang, text messaging, and so forth.

In addition, Textual ETL converts unstructured text into a structured format. The structured format is what is required in order for text to be processed in a query and analytical format by the computer. And unless the computer can process text in its own structured format, it cannot handle the volumes of data that the system must inspect.

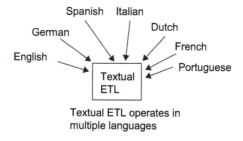

Textual ETL operates in multiple languages

Figure 14.8

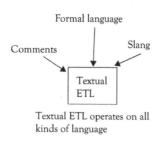

Textual ETL operates on all kinds of language

Figure 14.9

From Unstructured to Structured

Figure 14.10 shows that Textual ETL performs the service of converting unstructured data to structured data.

Another important service performed by Textual ETL, which is absolutely essential to a user, is to serve as a conduit from one technology to another. Figure 14.11 shows that Textual ETL allows electronically stored information such as e-mail communications to be transformed into any standard database format.

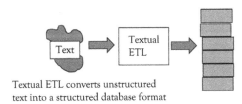

Textual ETL converts unstructured
text into a structured database format

Figure 14.10

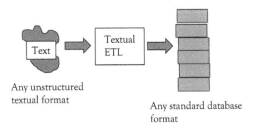

Any unstructured
textual format

Any standard database
format

Figure 14.11

CHAPTER 15

An Ophthalmology Analogy

So that's the overview from a computer-implementation perspective. But there's another way to look at all this from a distance. We've come up with an analogy. The world presents itself to our brain through our eyes. When we suspect that our vision of the world is less than it should be, we make an appointment with an eye doctor, professionally known as an ophthalmologist. Anyone who's visited such a physician (we resist typing the *o* word again) knows that an eye doctor, or an assistant, will deploy a number of devices to measure the efficacy of our eyes.

Approximately 75 percent of Americans (about 225 million people) use corrective lens of one kind or another.[1] Probably everyone is familiar with an eye chart, the one that has the big *E* at the top.

But in another test, to settle on a prescription, a device called a refractor is swung toward the eyes and sits over the bridge of the patient's nose. Patients never perceive a refractor in the way it's depicted below, because they're behind it and looking into it, but when the device is put in front of a patient, it looks the way it is shown in Figure 15.1.[2]

The patient looks at an eye chart in the distance with big E at the top, with either strings of letters or fragments of sentences in progressively smaller fonts. Then a series of lenses are swiveled into place. For each one, the person using the refractor asks the patient to close one eye and to report which lenses make his or her vision clearer.

When the different lenses are used, the patient is asked, "Which is better? No. 1 or No. 2?" "No. 3 or No. 4?" Anyone wearing prescription glasses will remember being presented with those choices.

So now we see that this analogy is close to the advance we have described in this book.

The patient is analogous to the user.

The refractor is analogous to the software capable of reading unstructured text.

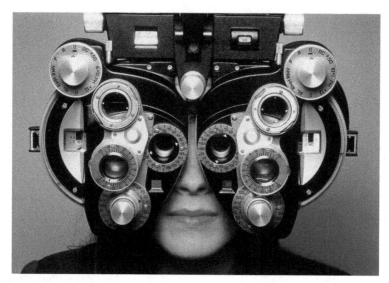

Figure 15.1 Refractor

The eye-doctor or technician operating the refractor is analogous to the in-house attorney using the software.

The various taxonomies (or controlled vocabularies or word clusters, if you prefer a different term) are analogous to the lenses that configure the software.

The big E eye chart (not shown) is analogous to the enterprise unstructured data such as e-mails, text messages, warranty claims and other customer complaints, and employee complaints.

Although no analogy is perfect, the patient-refractor-lenses-doctor-chart metaphor is a good way to understand the enterprise-software-training data-attorney-emails, etc. approach we have described to this point.

PART V

Proof of Concept

CHAPTER 16

Finding the Signal

Now, for the *product liability* use case, let's set the stage. When the computer era was in its early days, memos were paper documents. They were stored in file folders, which were in turn stored in filing cabinets. And back then, they were sometimes hard to find.

One famous example is the Ford Pinto Memo. The Pinto entered the marketplace in 1971. Two years later, two Ford engineers submitted a response to the National Highway Transportation Safety Administration, to which a memo was attached. The memo was entitled, *Fatalities Associated with Crash Induced Fuel Leakage and Fires.*[1] It was Ford's cost-benefit calculation that the value of a human life was less than an $11 part.[2]

The memo was not brought to light until it was featured in an article headlined "Pinto Madness," which appeared in the September to October 1977 issue of *Mother Jones.*[3] By then, over 2.3 million Pintos had been produced.[4]

Without getting into a debate on the merits of the case,[5] the point here is this: There was a four-year time lag between the memo's creation and the discovery of its significance. The memo is now famous and had an electric effect. It led to criminal charges, massively expensive lawsuits, and product recalls.

Suppose that in-house counsel sees a threat like the Pinto Memo and in an e-mail reminds top management of the company's *document retention* policies—a privileged attorney-client communication—and company personnel follows up by engaging in a massive *shredding* exercise during the midnight hours; except that the company doesn't use shredders, it uses deletion software.

Now suppose that, for whatever reason, the privilege applicable to the e-mail containing the *document retention* advice is either waived or deemed unworthy of the privilege under the crime or fraud *exception* to the attorney–client privilege. At a later trial, assuming the e-mail is accepted into evidence, that e-mail would likely have a persuasive effect on the jury.

It would be a mistake to believe that this scenario is entirely fictional. In fact, the trial of now–defunct Arthur Andersen in the context of the collapse of Enron involved similar facts.[6]

Now suppose two hiring managers are considering a candidate. From the relaxed environment of his desk, one manager learns that the candidate has sued her previous employer and also previously filed for bankruptcy. He writes an e-mail to the other, stating "Don't interview her. She is bad news. She sued a prior employer and has all kinds of financial problems."

What's wrong with this? Well, the employee has a case for failure to hire based on *protected activity*, where the protected activities are filing a lawsuit and filing for bankruptcy. Everyone is *entitled* to access the courts to redress a wrong or to take advantage of a statutory right. So the e-mail could turn into a *smoking gun.*[7]

The attorneys who seek to be hired by plaintiffs know to ask for e-mails in discovery. International Litigation Services (ILS), an eDiscovery vendor for attorneys who typically represent only plaintiffs, acknowledges that e-mails are *casual and candid.* In fact, ILS writes:

> For that reason, uncovering and obtaining all relevant e-mails is critical as part of a plaintiff electronic discovery plan against corporate defendants, as e-mail is often now more than ever the "smoking gun" in civil litigation.
>
> Over the last few years as electronic discovery case law has developed, it has become clear that e-mail correspondence contains not only relevant facts, but also crucial evidence for plaintiff trial attorneys. Unlike formal written correspondence, where the writer expects to disseminate the information and employs a certain "spin" on the facts, internal corporate e-mails often admit truths in an unequivocal manner.[8]

ILS goes on to give examples. In one case alleging overcharges, internal e-mails predicted a class action. In another case, e-mail threads from executives suggested that the company knew of the faulty equipment and failed to take remedial steps. In another case, a class action lawsuit, e-mails between the company and its marketing firm admitted that certain text messages were likely illegal.

Now, if what ILS says is not enough to persuade the corporate world about the impact of e-mails, consider what happened after *The Wall Street Journal* published just two of them. One e-mail, dated March 9, 2000, was written by a Merck research chief, and stated that cardiovascular incidents *are clearly there.* Another e-mail, written by a different Merck research executive, allegedly suggested that people at high risk be excluded from a trial so the rate of cardiovascular problems of Vioxx patients and others *would not be evident.*

So what happened? After these e-mails were published, Merck's stock dropped by over 10 percent, which represented a loss in valuation (at the time) of $6.9 billion.[9]

So it's easy to realize that it takes only one or two e-mails, or a damaging phrase in one of them, to support a lawsuit or to undermine a company's brand.[10]

But there are two other points to be made. First, to the extent that business people think that deletions are helpful, they need to be set straight. E-mails aren't just deleted. In fact, some advisors think of the *e* in e-mail as standing for *everlasting* or *eternal.* While a deletion may un-hook an e-mail's *address*, the e-mail data, structured and unstructured, is still there. So when a forensic expert finds deletions, the deletion serves only to tickle the nose of a bloodhound. Even when the e-mails are successfully deleted, a good forensic expert will find evidence of the deletion software that was used to do the dirty deed.

The second point is that e-mails are so yesterday. One example of a *new* e-mail is the text message. Although corporate employees (including executives) may have more discipline when writing e-mails these days, they may be casual and candid (to quote ILS) when sending text messages on their cell phones.

And for the younger generation, social media is the newer e-mail or, alternatively, the new text message. Are members of the younger generation even more cavalier with messages on social media sites than business professionals are with text messages? Review just about any teenager's post to Facebook and the answer is there: Yes; a resounding Yes.

All of this—e-mail content, text messages, social media posts—is unstructured textual information. But e-mails are still considered the place to look to find *intent*. For this reason, we used e-mails for a *proof of concept* with Textual ETL.

That's next.

CHAPTER 17

The Enron E-mails

How does any innovator find the courage to move forward with an inspiration to the point where an abstract idea becomes reality? When do we become the journalists of our own creation? Journalists ask the so-called Ws: Who, What, Where, When, Why, and How. We knew those questions were going to be asked.

We had to ask ourselves *Who*? Well, that was easy. We were the *Who*. We kept searching the Internet to find anyone else who had this *early warning* idea *plus* a methodology for implementing it. At the point when we decided to write this book, we had come up empty. We had found no other technology that we thought would work. In short, it was up to us.

We had to ask *What*? We knew the answer to that one, too. We were trying to bring *preventive law* back to life because we thought that computer science and technology had progressed to the point where we could revive it in the form of an early warning system that would help to prevent litigation.

In addition, we thought that we had found a strong business case for this and that a company would flourish; and, further, with a business case as a driver, we thought that our approach would forever change the way attorneys (at least in-house attorneys) practiced law. They would be the data lawyers; the new lawyers of the 21st century.

The question of *Where* was an easy one to answer. The United States is well-known around the world for being litigious. The answer was *here*, with the unfortunate caveat that the industrialized and industrializing nations are catching up.

The question of *When* was only a little harder. The era of Big Data had arrived and the business community saw that, in a customer-facing way, recommendation systems could drive revenue. More than a few entrepreneurs were getting some intelligence out of structured data, but few business leaders appreciated that *structured data* was the principal fountain of that intelligence, and that unstructured data, especially textual data, held so much more.

During the first quarter of 2014, Nick presented Bill with a challenge: Could he use the Enron e-mails, of which there are about 600,000, and a set of hot words to identify one or more e-mails where those hot words were within close proximity to one another, and report out those e-mails? So that was *When*.

And, of course we knew that we would have to prove that we could answer to the business community and to the legal community when they asked us *Why?*

With what we've said so far, we hope you're convinced that there is value in a system whose object is to seek out the *risk* of litigation in its own internal communications and to address that risk before it materializes into a lawsuit.

But then there was that nagging question, the one that really mattered: *How?* Did Bill have a solution that could be implemented to *drive results?*

That step is called the *proof of concept* (POC).

The challenge was to configure Textual ETL with business-relevant taxonomies (Bill used *General Business* and *Energy*), and then a small *hot word* set of only six words, and put it up against the Enron e-mails. He instructed Textual ETL to report out e-mails when it found two of the hot words within 100 bytes of each other.

Bill put his POC into a set of 47 PowerPoint slides and we show just one of them here in Figure 17.1.

What is Bill showing here? The point was *not* to uncover any of the specific e-mails that might have helped to sink Enron. The point was to separate the wheat from the chaff in order to get to the business-relevant e-mails, and then, more to the point, to find the hot words Bill selected within a given (and user-variable) separation.

In the slide in Figure 17.1, the separation was 100 bytes and Textual ETL found two of the hot words listed in the window in the upper *right* hand corner, namely *gas* and *oblige*.

Textual ETL reported that e-mail as an output in the upper *left* hand corner, with those two words highlighted in Figure 17.1.

It's the output that would be interesting to a user.

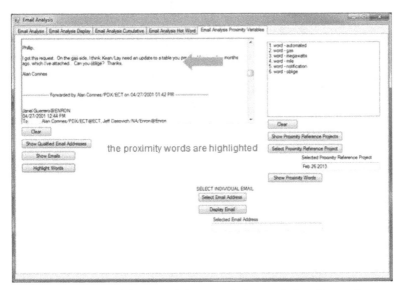

Figure 17.1 Textual ETL with hot words (top right) and e-mail output (top left)

Now, the Enron case was only an *alpha* test. The hot words were not germane to the accounting fraud that brought down Enron, and, after reading two books that told the Enron story, we didn't think we'd find any such e-mails. Still, it proves that the way forward is not an impossible task.

PART VI

Implementation

CHAPTER 18

The System to Prevent Litigation: Who Should Manage It, and Why

As we see it, in-house counsel will be in the forefront of a paradigm shift for lawyers. For this reason, which we believe is not yet appreciated, in-house attorneys will be more specialized and valuable in the future.

And precisely because of their expertise and proximity to communications within the enterprise, and received by the enterprise, the system we describe in this book must be instituted and controlled by the Legal Department, headed by the General Counsel (or the Chief Legal Officer), or by a law firm serving the company in that same capacity.[1]

For these reasons, we foresee that some portion of the IT staff will have to be dedicated to and under the supervision of the Legal Department. Accordingly, in-house counsel will necessarily have to learn more about the computer infrastructure, just as the IT staff will need to learn more about how to support the lawyers with whom they will be working.

In-house counsel may have to become familiar with Bill's software. Perhaps it will be the key to this revolution. But we wouldn't be intellectually honest if we ignored the recent development of Deep Learning, an aspect of machine learning, and a resurgence in Natural Language Processing (NLP), in both research and startup funding. After all, IBM debuted Watson in 2011 in the famous contest on *Jeopardy!* (see www.ibm.com/watson); Google is now also known for self-driving cars and acquired DeepMind in 2014 (see www.deepmind.com); and Microsoft announced Project Adam in July of 2014 and acquired Equivio in January of 2015. A startup called MetaMind was launched in December of 2014 (www.metamind.io), with $8 million in funding; and then there's Sentient Technologies (www.sentient.ai) which has so far raised $143 million. In fact, the venture capital firms have noticed the progress in AI research and invested almost $310 million in 2014, a far cry from the $15 million AI garnered in 2010.[2] This list of artificial intelligence platforms is not exhaustive and will likely grow.

But why are the Legal Department and in-house counsel so central to this process?

To explain, we should depict the process. It begins with configuring the software. In a generic sense, we now understand how to do that. In-house counsel should focus on how that step is done, propose hypotheticals, and consider data-mining the company's *legacy* litigation files (meaning closed cases). The accuracy and efficiency of the company's culture-specific early warning system will depend on this.

That's the first stage. In the graphic that follows, Figure 18.1, look for Start.

The process shifts to stage two when the system reports a threat. Then counsel must become an investigator and an analyst. Sherlock Holmes, if you will. Sherlock would ask: Who else is involved? And go from there, to interrogate the company's intranet and find the parent-child e-mails.

At some point, counsel might call off the investigation, or complete it and report to an executive who is a member of the company's control group. That interaction turns counsel into a strategist and planner. Working with a control group executive, the attorney can explore the variety of ways to address the threat.

Then that executive, having benefitted from the early warning and the advice of counsel, can take action, proactive action. Since executives in a control position are empowered to instruct counsel, the character that comes to mind is not Sherlock, the mystery solver, but Smokey the Bear and the iconic phrase, "Only *you* can prevent forest fires."

In Figure 18.1, you'll find the dataflow, but without Sherlock and Smokey. As you can see, the system has these four stages.

Now you can see *why* the system starts with an attorney in the Legal Department. By installing and controlling the system, in-house counsel will be able to oversee how the system is configured with the pertinent lenses, meaning the appropriate sentiments and the subject matter *hot words* that might reveal a specific type of threat.

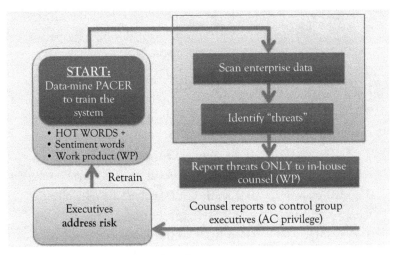

Figure 18.1 Intraspexion's dataflow

By installing and operating the system, the attorney's findings, advice, and counsel should be confidential under a combination of the attorney work-product doctrine and the attorney-client privilege.

Acting alone, management cannot achieve such confidentiality: "Privilege does not apply to 'an internal corporate investigation made by management itself.'"[3]

Let's be more precise. Some may wonder whether the system's findings could be subpoenaed as evidence to prove that the enterprise ignored the yellow light and should have known better. Our answer is no, we don't think so. In the typical case, the system is designed for confidentiality, and that discussion requires us to move into the legalistic waters of the attorney work-product doctrine and the attorney-client privilege. If you're not an attorney, it's time to learn something new.

The work-product doctrine should apply when the Legal Department installs the system, helps to configure it, and operates it when in-house attorneys investigate the *prospect* of litigation. The doctrine is a powerful cloak:

> Work-product protection is "broader than the attorney-client privilege." ... Rule 26(b)(3), which codifies the work-product protection, states in part that if a court orders discovery of materials prepared in anticipation of litigation by or for another party or its

representative, "it must protect against disclosure of the mental impressions, conclusions, opinions, or legal theories of a party's attorney or other representative concerning the litigation." Unlike the protection granted to attorney-client communications, "[t]he privilege derived from the work-product doctrine is not absolute." Like other qualified privileges, it may be overcome by a showing of substantial need.

The Second Circuit has interpreted the "in anticipation of litigation" requirement broadly. Documents should therefore be "deemed prepared in 'anticipation of litigation'" if "in light of the nature of the document and the factual situation in the particular case, the document can fairly be said to have been prepared or obtained because of the *prospect* of litigation."[4]

Then, when counsel reports to a control group executive, the communication should be confidential pursuant to the attorney-client privilege.

The attorney-client privilege is one of the oldest recognized privileges for confidential communications. The privilege is designed to "encourage full and frank communication between attorneys and their clients." The privilege serves the dual purpose of shielding "from discovery advice given by the attorney as well as communications from the client to the attorney, made in pursuit of or in facilitation of the provision of legal services." However, because the attorney-client privilege 'stands in derogation of the public's 'right to every man's evidence' … [i]t ought to be strictly confined within the narrowest possible limits consistent with the logic of the principle."

It is well settled that "[t]he burden of establishing the existence of an attorney-client privilege, in all of its elements, rests with the party asserting it. In order to prevail on an assertion of the attorney-client privilege the party invoking the privilege" must show that:

"(1) the asserted holder of the privilege is or sought to become a client; (2) the person to whom communication was made (a) is a member of the bar of a court, or his subordinate and

(b) in connection with this communication is acting as a lawyer; (3) the communication relates to a fact of which the attorney was informed (a) by his client (b) without the presence of strangers (c) for the purpose of securing primarily either (i) an opinion on law or (ii) legal services or (iii) assistance in some legal proceeding, and not (d) for the purpose of committing a crime or tort; and (4) the privilege has been (a) claimed and (b) not waived by the *client*."[5]

Ah, the *client*. Who speaks for the *client* when the client is a corporation? Under the control group test, a confidential communication between in-house counsel and a control group person should be privileged when the communication is not intended to perpetuate a crime or fraud, and the person is in a position to control or have a substantial role in determining what the corporation will do.

However, there is also a *subject matter* test. Under this test, an in-house attorney's advice is confidential when (i) the communication is made for the purpose of giving or receiving legal advice, (ii) the employee who is communicating with the attorney is doing so at the direction of a superior, (iii) the direction is given by the superior to obtain legal advice for the corporation, (iv) the subject matter of the communication is with the scope of the employee's duties, and (v) the communication is not disseminated beyond those persons who need to know.[6]

Now, suppose that a potential risk has been addressed. Is that it? No. The enterprise must learn from both its successes in preventing a potential lawsuit as well as from lawsuits that escape into reality. We don't have a failure. We have an opportunity. Just like Harold Brown said of his father in the Foreword, we have to ask what went wrong? When? We will learn how to guard against a future escapee probably in the same way that business professionals are learning how to avoid cyber attacks today.

And the persons who should reconfigure the system are, again, the in-house attorneys, assisted by and working with technology professionals under the attorneys' direction and control.

And when new cases or new legislation arises, the system can be updated by counsel, either by adding new *hot words* from an actual incident or by framing hypotheticals. The good news is that attorneys won't need training to frame hypotheticals, because law school professors use hypotheticals when they teach, and law students are trained to deal with them. As you may already know, attorneys are not unfamiliar with using hypotheticals in the arguments they frame.

Thus, given the tools and the willingness to converse with and learn from their IT colleagues, in-house counsel will be transformed into data lawyers. They will become analysts, investigators, and strategists. They will hunt for the bad facts that pose a risk of causing harm to the company, and in this respect, they will have power. They will have power because it is far easier to intercede as the facts are being developed than it is to change the applicable *laws*. The law, in its majesty, moves rather glacially compared to the speed we humans use when we create new facts.

Before moving on, there is one other point we would like to make.

Suppose the system indicates that an employee is being victimized in some way. More specifically, suppose the internal e-mails shows that an employee is being victimized by one of the discrimination torts. Should the human resources (HR) director bring up the matter with that person, who may be just *suffering through it*?

The answer is yes, because victims have a general duty to mitigate damages. In the context of a Title VII employment discrimination case, the U.S. Supreme Court put it this way:

> The requirement to show that the employee has failed in a coordinate duty to avoid or mitigate harm reflects an equally obvious policy imported from the general theory of damages, that a victim has a duty "to use such means as are reasonable under the circumstances to avoid or minimize the damages" that result from violations of the statute. *Ford Motor Co.* v. *EEOC*, 458 U.S. 219, 231, n. 15 (1982) (quoting C. McCormick, Law of Damages 127 (1935) (internal quotation marks omitted). An employer may, for example, have provided a proven, effective mechanism for reporting and resolving complaints of sexual harassment, available to the employee without undue risk or expense. If the plaintiff unreasonably failed to avail herself of

the employer's preventive or remedial apparatus, she should not recover damages that could have been avoided if she had done so. *If the victim could have avoided harm, no liability should be found against the employer who had taken reasonable care, and if damages could reasonably have been mitigated no award against a liable employer should reward a plaintiff for what her own efforts could have avoided.*[7]

Moreover, the Equal Opportunity Employment Commission (EEOC) has stated in a published Guidance that "if the respondent [employer] can prove that the complaining party [employee] failed to exercise reasonable diligence to mitigate his/her damages and could have avoided or minimized such damages with reasonable effort, the damages may be reduced accordingly."[8]

However, the employer has the burden to show that the employee failed to exercise reasonable diligence to mitigate damages. As the EEOC has put it:

- "the employer has the burden of showing that the plaintiff failed to make reasonable efforts to find work to mitigate her damages when seeking back pay;
- the burden is on the employer to prove, as an affirmative defense, that the employee failed to mitigate damages when seeking lost wages; and
- the employer has the burden of producing sufficient evidence to establish the amount of interim earnings or lack of diligence in mitigating damages on the part of the plaintiff."[9]

Accordingly, employees should appreciate this opportunity to mitigate past or present harm and an opportunity to avoid further harm. Every honest employee has a vested, personal interest in avoiding harm to himself or herself.

However, this general rule is not without exception. There are a few. In a recent EEOC case, a district court held that the EEOC was not required to prove that female employees, who allegedly had been groped, made reasonable efforts to limit their emotional harm caused by the alleged harassment:

> In the 1972 Amendments, Congress explicitly chose to include a duty of claimants to mitigate back pay losses. Pub. L. No. 92-261, 86 Stat. 103, 107 (1972). Congress' deliberate decision to carve out this duty to mitigate damages [for back pay losses] clearly signifies that Congress did not intend to create a duty to mitigate all compensatory damages. If Congress intended there to be a duty to mitigate all compensatory damages, it is illogical that it chose to single out the duty to mitigate back pay alone. Because this court relied on common law when faced with an evident statutory purpose, it committed clear error. Accordingly, reconsideration is appropriate and Title VII claimants do not have a duty to mitigate emotional damages.[10]

But would an HR Director feel comfortable getting involved in a situation like that? Would the allegedly groped employee be sensitive not only to being groped but to having anyone else know about it?

Now we come to the issue of privacy: What about that?

CHAPTER 19

The *No Privacy* Policies

We realize that employees often follow the practice of *bring your own devices* (BYOD) to work. While BYOD may be a common practice today, it is inadvisable for security *and preventive* purposes. Given the cost of remediating a hack into the enterprise's computer system, a company will want to protect itself from being hacked when a BYOD device is connected to the enterprise intranet. Because we want to identify and investigate what employees are saying to each other in order to be pro-active about potential litigation threats, we see BYOD as a significant and avoidable risk. But if a company adopts a BYOD policy, it can be implemented on devices in secure containers called Sand boxes (see https://en.wikipedia.org/wiki/Sandbox_(computer_Security)).

In addition, we hasten to say, we do not want a business to invade any employee's privacy when they have a reasonable expectation of having it. How do we navigate these waters?

What an Employer Should Do

We start with what a client should do, which is to have a *computer technology resource* (CTR) policy and to insist that each employee read and sign an Employee Manual that contains the CTR policy.

We do not mean to even suggest that we are giving legal advice, but we think the CTR policy might want to promulgate a policy something like the following:

1. Company computer and e-mail accounts should be used only for company business.
2. Employees are prohibited from sending or receiving personal e-mails, except when using a company computer to access a personal, password-protected, web-based e-mail account (for example,

a personal Yahoo, Google, or other e-mail account); provided, however, that if the use is so frequent and so extensive that the employee is found to be insufficiently inattentive to his or her work, or disrupts the business operations of others, then the employee may be either disciplined or terminated.

3. Employees have no right to privacy with respect to any personal information or messages created on or accessed using a company computer or e-mail account.

4. E-mails sent or received on company computer resources are not private and should be regarded as postcards, and should not be understood as the equivalent of a sealed letter.

5. The company may inspect all files or messages on company computer resources at any time, for any reason, at its discretion.

6. The company or its agents may periodically monitor its computer resources and e-mail accounts to ensure compliance with its CTR policies.

7. If any of the foregoing provisions are found to be against public policy or are unlawful, then any and all such provisions are severed from the Employee Manual, but the rest of the CTR policies and provisions shall remain in effect.

Why these elements? Because if a company follows this set of mandates, disclosures, and warnings, then, if there is no deviation from them, not even an employee's communication *with his or her personal attorney* will be entitled to privacy or privileged from discovery by the company.

Can this be? Surely the attorney-client privilege would apply to keep an employee's communication with his or her attorney privileged from disclosure, wouldn't it? The answer, if the above-listed CTR policies are in place, at least in California, is *no*.

In *Holmes v. Petrovich Development Co., LLC*,[1] the appellate court noted that when the employer has an express policy that reduces any expectation of privacy, e-mail communications between an employee and her attorney may be equivalent to "consulting her lawyer in her employer's conference room, in a loud voice, with the door open."

Gina M. Holmes worked as an executive assistant for the defendants Paul Petrovich and Petrovich Development Company LLC. After she was hired, she read and signed the company's express CTR policy that governed her usage of the company computer and e-mail account. It stated the elements we have described previously.

In July 2004, approximately one month after Holmes was hired, she told Petrovich she was pregnant and wanted to take a six week maternity leave in December. She later revised her request to a four month maternity leave beginning in November. This prompted Petrovich to send the following e-mail to Holmes:

> I need some honesty. How pregnant were you when you interviewed with me and what happened to six weeks? . . . That is an extreme hardship on me, my business and everyone else in the company. You have rights for sure and I am not going to do anything to violate any laws, but I feel taken advantage of and deceived for sure.

Holmes was offended and e-mailed a response that explained she did not tell him about her pregnancy earlier, in part, because she had two miscarriages in the past and did not want to disclose the pregnancy until it appeared likely that she would carry the baby to term.

Because Petrovich was concerned that Holmes may be quitting, he forwarded Holmes' e-mail to human resources and in-house counsel. When Holmes learned that Petrovich forwarded her e-mails to others, she was upset and sought legal advice concerning a claim for pregnancy discrimination.

For example, Holmes exchanged several e-mails with her attorney from her company e-mail account where she stated:

> I know that there are laws that protect pregnant women from being treated differently due to their pregnancy, and now that I am officially working in a hostile environment, I feel I need to find out what rights, if any, and what options I have. I don't want to quit my job; but how do I make the situation better?

This e-mail conflicted with Holmes's contentions at trial. At trial, her counsel objected when Petrovich's counsel tried to introduce this e-mail and other e-mails like it.

The trial court *overruled* the objections, the e-mails were admitted into evidence, and the Court of Appeals *affirmed*, holding that the employer's computer policy made clear that Holmes had no legitimate reason to believe that communications from her company e-mail account were private, regardless of whether the employer actually monitored her e-mail.

Thus, given the CTR policy, Holmes was held to have knowingly disclosed her attorney-client communications to her employer and *waived* the privilege.

Holmes is a 2011 California decision. In 2007, a New York court reached a similar conclusion. In *Scott v. Beth Israel Med. Ctr.*, the e-mail policy stated:

> This Policy clarifies and codifies the rules for the use and protection of the Medical Center's computer and communications systems. This policy applies to everyone who works at or for the Medical Center including employees, consultants, independent contractors, and all other persons who use or have access to these systems.
>
> 1. All Medical Center computer systems, telephone systems, voice mail systems, facsimile equipment, electronic mail systems, Internet access systems, related technology systems, and the wired or wireless networks that connect them are the property of the Medical Center and should be used for business purposes only.
>
> 2. All information and documents created, received, saved or sent on the Medical Center's computer or communications systems are the property of the Medical Center.
>
> Employees have no personal privacy right in any material created, received, saved, or sent using Medical Center communications or computer systems. The Medical Center reserves the right to access and disclose such material at any time without prior notice.[2]

The policy was available in hard copy and maintained in the office of the administrator for each of the Center's departments and on the intranet.

The plaintiff, Dr. Scott, was the chairman of the orthopedics department and worked closely with the department administrator.

In 2002, every employee received an employee handbook that contained a brief summary of the e-mail policy. After 2002, newly hired doctors were required to sign a form acknowledging that they had read and were familiar with it.

However, Dr. Scott never signed such an acknowledgment and denied knowing of it.

Nevertheless, this *no personal use* policy, combined with a policy allowing for employer monitoring and the employee's knowledge of these two policies, diminished any expectation of privacy.

The issue materialized when Dr. Scott used Center computers to communicate by e-mail with his counsel. When Dr. Scott asserted the attorney-client privilege, the Center rejected his claim to the privilege, citing the policy.

So Dr. Scott sought a protective order from the court, but the court denied it.

In denying Dr. Scott's request for a protective order, the court cited a federal bankruptcy case, which held that the attorney-client privilege was inapplicable if:

1. "... the corporation maintain[s] a policy banning personal or other objectionable use,
2. ... the company monitor[s] the use of the employee's computer or e-mail,
3. ... third parties have a right of access to the computer or e-mails, and
4. ... the corporation notif[ies] the employee, or the employee was aware, of the use and monitoring policies."[3]

In *Scott*, the court found that the first two elements were satisfied by the Center's *no personal use* and monitoring policies; found the third element inapplicable; and held that Dr. Scott had both actual and constructive notice of the policy because the policy had been disseminated to each employee in 2002, including Dr. Scott, and because the Center made the policy available by notice on the Center's intranet.

In addition, because Dr. Scott was an administrator, he was held to have constructive notice of the policy, in part because he required newly hired doctors under his supervision to acknowledge in writing that *they* were aware of it.

As a final matter, the court rejected the argument that the attorney's notice in its e-mails to Dr. Scott changed the outcome. The notice stated:

> "This message is intended only for the use of the Addressee and may contain information that is privileged and confidential. If you are not the intended recipient, you are hereby notified that any dissemination of this communication is strictly prohibited. If you have received this communication in error, please erase all copies of the message and its attachments and notify us immediately."

This (not atypical) notice appeared in every e-mail from counsel to Dr. Scott. However, the court held that the notice could not create a right of privacy out of whole cloth and did not alter the Center's policy stating: "When client confidences are at risk, [counsel's] pro forma notice at the end of the e-mail is insufficient and not a reasonable precaution to protect its clients." (For this reason, an early warning system should be configured to ignore this pro forma notice in internal communications.)

What an Employer Should *Not* Do

Given its long and venerable history, no employer should expect courts to frequently hold that the attorney-client privilege has been waived.

Undermine the Policy by Conduct

However, actions often speak louder than words. Suppose that a company had a CTR policy identical to the policy described in *Petrovich*.

But now suppose that the company sent the message that noncompliance would be *tolerated*. That message undermines the policy, and it is known as *operational reality*.

The *operational reality* test is used in the Ninth Circuit and was discussed in a 2008 opinion, *Quon v. Arch Wireless Operating Co.*[4]

In *Quon*, the plaintiff had a reasonable expectation of privacy as to his personal text messages sent from his company pager because of an informal policy that contradicted the written policy. The plaintiff's supervisor had made it clear that text messages would not be audited if employees paid any applicable overage charges, even though the employer's policy prohibited the personal use of pagers.

In other words, the *operational reality* was that the plaintiff had a reasonable expectation that his personal text messages would be kept private. Thus, under those circumstances, an informal policy effectively voided the written policy.

Why can we have some confidence in the CTR policy in *Holmes*? Because Holmes actually argued that she had a reasonable expectation that her e-mails to her attorney were private because of the *operational reality* that the company did not audit employee computers during her employment.

But that argument failed. The Court of Appeal rejected it because there was no evidence that the company had an informal policy that contradicted its express, written policy.

So the message is fairly clear. If a company promulgates a written policy, no supervisor should undercut it with a verbal policy to the contrary.

Permit Employees to Use Personal Computer Resources for Work

Holmes also argued that she had a reasonable expectation of privacy, because she used a private password for her company e-mail account and deleted the e-mails after they were sent. The Court also rejected this argument because Holmes utilized her *company* e-mail account, not her *personal* e-mail account.

But suppose that the CTR policy is not clear, and an employee uses a company computer to access a personal, password-protected, web-based e-mail system to communicate with his or her attorney.

A New Jersey appellate court addressed these facts in 2010.[5] There, the plaintiff used her company issued laptop to access her Yahoo account to e-mail her attorney about bringing an employment discrimination lawsuit against her employer. The company CTR policy had *not* prohibited this.

Not surprisingly, the New Jersey court held that the attorney-client privilege had *not* been waived.

Moreover, the New Jersey court noted that a policy permitting an employer to retrieve and read an employee's attorney-client communications accessed on a *personal*, password-protected e-mail account would not be enforceable because, in New Jersey, it would be void as a matter of public policy.

Fail to Have Employees Read and Sign the Policy

Courts are reluctant to create exceptions to the attorney-client privilege, so hiccups in implementing a CTR policy can matter and change the outcome of a case. In *Mintz v. Mark Bartelstein & Assoc., Inc.*, *Holmes* was distinguished by the Court, and was *not* followed because *the employee did not read or sign the Employment Manual.*[6] *Holmes* was also distinguished because the plaintiff used his *home computer*, not a company device.[7] Evidently, there were no grounds for holding the employee to constructive notice, as in *Scott*.

Under the circumstances, the Court's ruling that Mintz had not waived his attorney-client privilege was not unexpected. Without requiring Mintz to read or sign the policy, and because there was no showing that Mintz had some supervisory capacity that would have made him aware of it, he could not be held to it.

The Internet of Things

Employers have been requiring employees to sign No Privacy policies since 2002, if not before. But the Internet of Things—the IoT—did not exist in 2002. Now the future is clear: The world will be populated with billions of smart, embedded computer devices that interact with our personal lives, *and interact with each other*. That's the IoT.

Thus, one of the subjects of the CTR Policy must be the devices that people, in their private lives, use to access their own personal data. The focus is not the data such devices access from the environment, that is, the weather conditions, which is not personal to them. The focus is the data such devices access from their own bodies, for example, such as smartphones or watches or other kinds of wearable devices that measure temperature, blood pressure, and so forth.[8] Such data is personal, private, and confidential to the persons who wear or otherwise carry them.

Any sensible person would see the difference between the data collected by such personal (and so private) devices and the enterprise computer ecosystem.

But, clearly, there is a potential for the personal device to exchange data with an enterprise device.

And so we have put our finger on a two-way street: The IoT opens a potential doorway for the enterprise to learn about an employee's otherwise personal information, and it also opens a path for the enterprise to open itself up to a hacker attack. We can't think of a better reason for a CTR policy to ban devices known as BYODs.

So, to protect privacy as well as to protect the enterprise, employees should be able to use approved devices furnished by the company, but should not be permitted to use their personal devices for work.

The Federal Trade Commission

There is yet another reason to have a CTR policy. In the context of an enterprise interacting with its customers, the Federal Trade Commission (FTC) has recently asserted a broad authority to protect the consumer. The legislation that created the FTC prohibits "unfair or deceptive acts or practices in or affecting commerce," and enables the FTC as a regulatory, enforcing agency, 15 U.S.C. 45(a). The law defines *unfair acts or practices* as acts or practices that cause or are likely to cause "substantial injury to consumers which [are] not reasonably avoidable by consumers themselves and not outweighed by countervailing benefits to consumers or to competition."[9]

For example, in a recent case, which was resolved by settlement, the FTC filed an enforcement action against TRENDNet, which makes routers, Internet cameras, and other networking devices.

The FTC alleged that TRENDNet had failed to adequately secure its Internet camera devices, which could have permitted users' live video streams to be exposed to the public. The adverse results were the litigation costs (of course), but also a requirement mandating TRENDNet to revise its security policies and the imposition of mandatory third-party reviews of its security obligations for the next 20 years.

In addition, there were restrictions on TRENDNet's marketing and its customer support obligations.

So a *trend* is clear.[10] Businesses can expect that a failure to adopt a privacy policy (at least in the context of the data it collects from consumers), or worse, a failure to abide by its own policies, may be seen as an *unfair and deceptive act* under the law.

Accordingly, businesses should, in addition to advising their engineers to secure the devices, have a CTR policy in order to demonstrate that it had a policy that was reasonable and that it had been implemented.

CHAPTER 20

How to Configure the System

Now that we've talked about why we think the Legal Department should be installing and operating an early warning system, let's go back to Figure 18.1, and the START of the data flow. We have to *configure* the software before we deploy it. That's what we mean by *Start*.

We've said that we use the word *taxonomies* to mean associative (not hierarchical) taxonomies or controlled vocabularies, and even word clusters if you prefer that terminology, but we'd like to start this chapter by discussing two other search methodologies, starting with the use of key words. In the early 1970s, the companies who were the publishers of court cases in paper form saw the value of a digital alternative. Law librarians began the process of learning for themselves and then teaching faculty and students how to login and then how to search the electronic legal databases using Boolean connectors, such as *and*, *or*, *not*, and so on.

Key words are still used, but times have changed.

In 2003, researchers at the University of California at Berkeley published an update to their study, "How Much Information?" At that point in time (and now hopelessly outdated), they explained that each year almost 800 megabytes of recorded information was produced per person, and that 92 percent of that information was stored on computers or a computer-based storage system. Eight hundred megabytes is enough to fill a set of books stacked 30 feet high.

Today, if each person generated only 25 percent more electronically stored information (ESI) than in 2003, or 1,000 megabytes, then each person would generate a gigabyte of data per year, and that amount is roughly equivalent to 75,000 pages, if printed.

It is easy to imagine that today we generate much more than that. Indeed, it is often said that 98 percent or 99 percent of all the information generated today, by everyone in the world, is generated as ESI. Why? Because today the digital universe includes not only servers, desktops, laptops, cell phones, hard drives, flash drives, and photocopy or fax or scan and e-mail machines, the digital universe includes data from TV and radio transmissions, telephone calls received as e-mails (or which are transcribed), surveillance cameras, datacenters supporting cloud computing, and, of course, social networks.

So, in lawsuits, parties and attorneys must often deal not just with gigabytes of data, but with terabytes of data, and a single terabyte is roughly equivalent to 75 million pages, if printed. Even if a requesting party asks for readily accessible data, meaning data in native format with metadata intact, there is still the problem of how to search through a much, much bigger haystack than lawyers ever faced when, for example, 10,000 boxes of documents were produced and made available in any number of warehouses.

Now, can anyone get their arms around this much data? No, they can't. The volume of data today is far greater than those times when parties attempted to hide the needle in the haystack by producing truckloads, or worse, warehouses full of boxes stuffed with papers.

In 2006, the federal judiciary recognized the problem, and enacted a set of litigation rules pertaining to the discovery of electronically stored information (ESI). The great state of California did not enact similar rules until 2009.

With ESI and rules for the discovery of potentially relevant information, technology had invaded the practice of law—in a big way—and it had done so right in the middle of every lawsuit.

So the companies in the business of copying documents either went out of business or migrated into the world of eDiscovery. Then an industry of eDiscovery vendors arose, and a work flow process was developed. That process is called the Electronic Discovery Reference Model (EDRM).

Generally speaking, the EDRM describes a conceptual work flow for the discovery phase of an existing lawsuit.[1]

Initially, the EDRM did not include Information Governance. However, more recently, Information Governance has been added, and there is a companion Information Governance Reference Model now.

This world of eDiscovery is partly the domain of an information technologist and partly the domain of lawyers. We've talked about e-mails, and you already know that, on occasion, people inside business organizations send copies of their e-mails to their colleagues. Do we need to add the *copies* to the pile of potentially relevant documents? No. So the technologist's initial approach was to cull the data by removing the duplicates. This was called *de-duping*. Do we need to look at the system files? No, so the system files were removed (*culled*) as well. De-duping and culling reduced the amount of the data.

But the *gold standard* was (and for many, still is) attorney review.[2] Attorneys were supposed to see each document on a monitor and tag them, generally into three categories:

- Potentially relevant;
- Potentially relevant but privileged from disclosure by the attorney work product doctrine or the attorney-client privilege; and
- Not relevant.

That process of attorney review and tagging was mind-numbing, and it eventually led to a business called legal process outsourcing (LPO). With LPO, the idea was to break a very large problem into a multiplicity of smaller ones. To do so, highly educated, English-speaking attorneys in other countries were provided with a monitor and a subset of the documents to be reviewed and tagged before they were produced. There were rows and rows of such attorneys.

LPO was, in effect, labor arbitrage. Such attorneys charged lower rates per hour, and were grateful for the work. But as the volume increased, not even rooms and rows of such attorneys was always cost-effective.

Enter statistical sampling. Now, in fact, the EDRM has been supplemented to recognize these changes as well, this time with a Computer Assisted Review Reference Model.[3]

What happened to key words? By themselves, in the face of so much data, they were discredited. Why?

Well, let's see. Test yourself. Here's the assertion: Key words using Boolean connectors will find less than 25 percent of the potentially relevant documents. True or false?

We won't give you the answer immediately. So please don't read ahead.

In 1985, David C. Blair and M. E. Maron, early pioneers in the *information retrieval* field, designed an experiment. We'll describe it with an analogy. Suppose there was a lake stocked with fish of various kinds. In this lake, there was a known subset of fish, which we'll call *goldfish*. The goldfish were in the lake, but there were only so many of them. In a fishing contest, the object was to pull up as many goldfish as possible. Pulling up a goldfish was a hit. Pulling up some other fish was a miss.

In other words, there was a small but known subset of relevant documents in the data lake.

Blair and Maron asked different teams of attorneys to use their most powerful key word search techniques to fish for and find the goldfish, the subset of relevant documents.[4]

What they learned was that the attorneys were overestimating the efficacy of their searches. The attorneys thought they were identifying 75 percent of the goldfish, but they were wrong: they were finding only about 20 percent.[5]

This study was conducted in 1985, so information scientists have known for decades that a key word search was a very porous net.

Recent results are, today, not much better. Studies show that key word searches are only a little more successful. Tomlinson and others reported in 2008 that Boolean key word searches identified only 22 percent of the relevant documents,[6] while Oard and others reported in 2009 that Boolean searches pinned only 24 percent of the potentially relevant documents.[7]

The problem is that key word searches depend on being able to search a large dataset for a specific word. But a key word search will not return a document if the specific word is not *in* that document. If a plaintiff always describes the death of a child as a *tragedy* and then has to turn over e-mails to the defense, and the defense looks for e-mails with the word *accident*, the key word search for *accident* will be fruitless.

While we humans may understand the similarity, and make the contextual leap, a computer *sees* only one string of ones and zeros for the request *accident* and is scanning the data for a matching string. Since the ones and zeros for *tragedy* don't match the ones and zeros for *accident*, the result will be *no documents found*.

But in 1977, a new and different approach was invented. It was called Latent Semantic Analysis or Latent Semantic Indexing.[8] But, really, it's simple: Latent means *hidden* and Semantic means *meaning*; or, in a phrase, *hidden meaning*.

This approach involved converting *documents* into digital form; in effect, digitizing the words on a per-document basis.

To get the idea, consider an imaginary spreadsheet. Across the top, and going horizontally, the documents are listed. So, for example, the document in the upper left hand corner of the spreadsheet is D1.

Then, imagine going vertically down from the column headed D1, and put in all of the words. List them vertically. So if Word 1 (W1) is in Document 1 (D1), we put a 1 in the cell created by D1–W1. That's the beginning.

Then the next document would be D2, and all the words in it would be listed vertically in that column. But now suppose that W1 is *not* in D2. Now we have our second cell: It's D2–W1. But in that cell, we write a 0. Word 1 (W1) is not in Document 2 (D2).

And so on.

Eventually, a giant spreadsheet comes into being; a Word-Document spreadsheet or, for the mathematically inclined, a Word-Document *matrix*. You can safely imagine that such a matrix is very large: If you had 100,000 documents with only 10 words in each document, you would create a spreadsheet of 100,000 columns and 10 rows. The number of cells, with all those ones and zeros is $100,000 \times 10 = 1$ million cells. A spreadsheet with 100,000 documents, each with only 1,000 words per document, is a spreadsheet with 100 million cells.

So fishing in that sea with key words is not likely to be productive. The great advance of this *hidden meaning* approach is that, in some cases, the words in one document will *co-occur* with the words in another document. So our key word search for *accident* might turn up a potentially relevant document even if the word *accident* is *not* present, because there are a sufficiently high number of other, *co-occurring* words in another document.[9] Documents with a high score of co-occurring words might be returned to a user making a key word search request even if the key word is *missing*.

Imagine that.

But where there is a global understanding of how the terms should be categorized, taxonomies are another useful and commonplace way of organizing information. There are many kinds of taxonomies.[10] One kind is the sort you might remember from a science class in high school: the hierarchical taxonomy. You've probably seen this kind of taxonomy in connection with biology. There are general terms (mammals, reptiles) and then narrower terms, and still narrower terms after that: A nest of terms.

Hierarchical taxonomies are *not* the only sort of taxonomies in use today. Some use related terms called *associative* taxonomies,[11] a distinction which we will explain in the next chapter.

CHAPTER 21

A Product Liability Example

What do we mean by associational taxonomies? We mean key words used in clusters. But these *word clusters* must relate to a specific topic. Such word clusters are sometimes called a *bag of words*.

Our best illustration is a recent one. We begin by choosing NOS code 365, the topic for personal injury: product liability. We'll want to construct a word cluster for this topic.

You may recall that General Motors (GM) had more than a little trouble early in 2014 pertaining to ignition switch defects. According to the Consent Decree in the matter, the defects showed up "in 619,122 model year (MY) 2005–2007 Chevrolet Cobalt and MY 2007 Pontiac G5 vehicles."[1]

In fact, "748,024 vehicles contain[ed] the same safety-related defect. Those additional vehicles are the MY 2006–2007 Chevrolet HHR and Pontiac Solstice, MY 2003–2007 Saturn Ion, and MY 2007 Saturn Sky vehicles."[2]

Moreover, GM indicated that service parts with the same defects were in another 823,788 vehicles. For these reasons, GM was obligated to recall 2,190,934 vehicles.[3]

The problem was massive, and all of the defects pertained to the ignition switch in these vehicles, the details of which are not important here.[4]

But when GM entered into a Consent Decree with the National Highway Traffic Safety Administration (NHTSA), a division of the U.S. Department of Transportation, to resolve the matter of failing to timely notify NHTSA, GM obligated itself to conduct recalls, pay a fine, and disavow how its attorneys trained its engineers.

The recalls were not small, and "affect[ed] a total population of 2,190,934 vehicles in the United States."[5]

The fine was large, too. GM agreed to pay $35 million, the maximum civil penalty, in addition to other financial penalties.[6]

The human cost was horrific. By May, 2015, a program to compensate victims had identified 97 deaths linked to the flawed switch.[7]

Of course, there was a ton of adverse publicity.

But wait, it gets worse. What's relevant here is what went generally unnoticed by the media, except for *Wall Street Journal* blogger Tom Gara, and one or two others. It turns out that a culture of safety did not exist at GM.

So, in paragraph 20 of the Consent Order, which Gara quoted in his blog article, there was this:

20. GM has initiated efforts to improve employee training regarding proper documentation practices and to encourage discussion of safety issues, including discussion of defects and safety consequences of defects. Such training will expressly *disavow* statements diluting the safety message in the nature of certain statements in pages 33–44 of the *attached Exhibit B.* (Italics added.)[8]

Disavow. So what was it in Exhibit B that GM was ordered to (and consented to) *disavow?*

It turns out that, in 2008, GM's attorneys had advised and instructed its engineers how to conceal the problems its engineers had seen. The attorneys didn't want those problems to turn into smoking guns. But Exhibit B, the attorneys' PowerPoint presentation, did.

The headline for Gara's blog was, "The 69 Words You Can't Use at GM." You can put that headline into any standard search engine. Gara's blog article will come up.

The 69 words were on screenshots of GM's attorneys' PowerPoint presentation to GM's engineers. The presentation will convey to you what we mean by a *cluster* of related (not hierarchical) words and phrases, which, in this case, serves to indicate a serious product liability risk (of any sort, not just defective ignition switches).

In one slide, GM's attorneys were quoting phrases which, in their opinion, were deemed *not* helpful to identify and solve problems. Here are the phrases GM's attorneys' didn't like:

- "This is a lawsuit waiting to happen ..."
- "Unbelievable Engineering screw up ..."
- "This is a safety and security issue ..."
- "This is a very dangerous thing to happen. My family refuses to ride in the vehicle now ..."
- "Scary for the customer ..."
- "Kids and wife panicking over the situation ..."
- "I believe the wheels are too soft and weak and could cause a serious problem ..."
- "Dangerous ... almost caused accident."

All of these slides express negative sentiments. The strongest negative sentiments, especially when understood in context, point to potential injury and expensive lawsuits in the making.

In another slide, GM's attorneys created a *word rug* under which potential smoking guns could be swept, the goal of which was to replace the smoking guns with words having more positive sentiment. GM's engineers were advised not to write *problem*, but to write *issue, condition,* or *matter* instead. Instead of *safety*, the engineers were advised to write *has potential safety implications*.

Instead of *judgmental words*, the engineers were to write *above* or *below* or *exceeds specification*. And instead of *defect* or *defective*, the engineers were directed to write *does not perform to design*.

And in yet another slide, GM's attorneys came up with a list of words that were "[s]ome examples of words or phrase that are to be avoided ...." Gara listed those words and phrases in his blog, and we will recount them here:

always, annihilate, apocalyptic, asphyxiating, bad, Band-Aid, big time, brakes like an X car, cataclysmic, catastrophic, Challenger, chaotic, Cobain, condemns, Corvair-like, crippling, critical, dangerous, deathtrap, debilitating, decapitating, defect, defective, detonate, disemboweling, enfeebling, evil, eviscerated, explode, failed, flawed, genocide, ghastly, grenadelike, grisly, gruesome, Hindenburg, Hobbling, Horrific, impaling, inferno, Kevorkianesque, lacerating, life-threatening, maiming, malicious, mangling, maniacal, mutilating, never, potentially disfiguring, powder keg, problem, rolling sarcophagus (tomb or coffin), safety, safety related, serious, spontaneous combustion, startling, suffocating, suicidal, terrifying, Titanic, unstable, widow-maker, words or phrases with a biblical connotation, [and] you're toast.[9]

Now, if you believe that people really *do* learn from their previous mistakes and that this message can be effectively *disavowed* by attending compliance seminars or in any other way, let us take issue with that proposition now. We don't believe it. There is a reason for the sayings that "Leopards don't change their spots" and "What's past is prologue."[10] Company cultures are hard to change.

In GM's case, of course, it is still burdened with its own past. While still a great institution, that past includes the Corvair and the 1999 verdict for $4.9 billion in connection with the gas tank of a 1979 Chevy Malibu that exploded after being rear-ended by a drunk driver.[11] In that one instance, six passengers were severely burned.[12]

Yet in 2008, GM's engineers were told not to use the 69 words we have recounted, even after those horrific and haunting (physically and financially) episodes.

But these words and phrases are just the sort we want our e-mail scanning software to find. And while GM was ordered to disavow its teachings, *we* can use these words—and their synonyms and still other words—to create an associative taxonomy of words that typify a product liability threat, at least in the automotive industry.

For preventive law purposes, we have learned from GM's unfortunate example, but we also remember the Challenger disaster and numerous others, and we can generalize. Where words of safety (or insufficient data) collide with words of money (as in the cost is too high, or there's not enough money left to do needed studies) or time (as in there's not enough time, or there have already been too many delays), we have no difficulty in predicting that there is a disaster (and a lawsuit) in the making.

In the product liability context, there are three prevention opportunities: (1) see and address the defective condition before it leaves the manufacturer's hands; (2) learn the risks by analyzing the warranty claims submitted by the customers; and (3) be proactive about damages, to eliminate or mitigate them with notices and, if necessary, recalls.

But in order to do any of this, in-house counsel needs a tool for understanding context and meaning of the unstructured text, and to have an opportunity to analyze it. Here, Bill has described his way to see this unstructured textual data.

Bill discounts Natural Language Processing (NLP).[13] But some form of NLP may provide a solution, and the recent appearance of Deep Learning cannot be dismissed with the wave of our hands. It is new and has attracted a lot of interest. While this particular form of NLP is beyond the scope of this book, it is certainly worth exploring. For example, the words and phrases in the GM example could be turned into a training corpus for a Deep Learning algorithm for a product liability vector space, which (in terms of our analogy) would be a lens or a filter. Time will tell. For now, we have to avoid our own biases and say that the jury is still out. As we write, neither approach has been turned into a product.

CHAPTER 22

Employment Discrimination

Instead of product liability, suppose the category of previous lawsuits of a certain type is the category of employment discrimination. Do we have enough data to create either associative taxonomies or NLP training sets for them? Yes. In the following data, we can see that there were 14,834 cases in Nature of Suit (NOS) code 442 in 2011, 14,307 cases in 2012, and 12,346 cases in 2013.

But the high water mark for these cases was further back in time. Here's the longer view:

NOS Code 442

Civil Rights—Employment

No. of Cases Filed Between January 01 and December 31 in Each Year

2000	20,116
2001	20,113
2002	20,172
2003	19,537
2004	18,818
2005	15,527
2006	13,555
2007	17,712
2008	12,993
2009	13,727
2010	14,598
2011	14,834
2012	14,307
2013	12,346
2014	11,900

Now, even though the trend is down, which is good, the numbers each year are still high. And, of course, factual allegations were made in each of the almost 12,000 or more cases that were filed in each and every year. If we focus only on the last five years, we would have almost 70,000 cases to review.[1]

So there's plenty of data. Will we have to download all of it, divide a year's worth of cases up into subcategories, and create the *hot words* associated with each of them? No. The truth is, we don't need to do so much work. To be confident that the *hot words* we select will accurately reflect each subcategory with a 95 percent confidence level and a 2.5 percent margin of error, we need slightly less than 1,600 cases in each subcategory.[2]

Because we described a starter set for a product liability taxonomy of hot words, we won't repeat the discussion for the workplace discrimination subcategories. The statistical approach is the same.

CHAPTER 23

The Government Provides an Example

In mid-October of 2014, the Securities and Exchange Commission (SEC) brought its first action against a *high-frequency* trading firm for manipulating stock closing prices. A *high-frequency* trading firm trades shares of stock in small fractions of a second. Talk about speed.

Because of that speed, some very computer-savvy people at Athena Capital Research LLC (Athena) thought that they could manipulate the stock market to their advantage.

In the SEC's Order in the case, the *relevant period* of this manipulation took place during the six months between June and December of 2009. It took five years to find the data and then to understand what Athena had been doing.

When Athena was faced with (1) the data and (2) their e-mails, they accepted an *offer of settlement*, agreed to pay a civil penalty of $1 million, and, without admitting or denying any of the findings, agreed to *cease and desist*.

But how the SEC came to understand what Athena was doing is a story relevant to the one we tell here. Short and simple, the SEC used *Big Data* techniques to search Athena's transactional (structured) data for a pattern that appeared to be suspicious. That data was public information, but it was not easy to find. The suspicious pattern was appearing during the last *two seconds* of trading on nearly every trading day during the relevant six-month period.

Having found a suspicious pattern, the SEC decided to exercise one of its powers and issued subpoenas for Athena's e-mails.

Once the SEC investigators received the e-mails, they began to understand the trading patterns in the context of the intentions expressed in the e-mails. Athena's intentions were only thinly disguised. The code name of their algorithm was *Gravy*, and, among other things, Athena was *marking the close*, meaning that they were buying and selling near the close of trading to affect the closing price, and was *owning the game*.

According to SEC's Order in the case, in the affected stocks, Athena's trades amounted to 70 percent of the transactions that took place during those last few seconds before the market closed. That volume overwhelmed the market's liquidity and pushed the market price, and therefore the closing price, in Athena's favor.

The Order is detailed, and we think the story is worth telling in the way the SEC told it. In the text below, we quote extensively from the Order. Because the e-mails revealed Athena's intent, the SEC's Order calls attention to them by putting some of the trading times and portions of the e-mails in **boldface**. The words in boldface are in the Order as it was written. The parenthetical phrase (*emphasis added*) is also in the Order and was not put there by us.

The following is the SEC's Order.*

UNITED STATES OF AMERICA
Before the
SECURITIES AND EXCHANGE COMMISSION

SECURITIES EXCHANGE ACT OF 1934
Release No. 73369 / October 16, 2014

INVESTMENT ADVISERS ACT OF 1940
Release No. 3950 / October 16, 2014

ADMINISTRATIVE PROCEEDING
File No. 3-16199

---

* http://www.sec.gov/litigation/admin/2014/34-73369.pdf

In the Matter of
**ATHENA CAPITAL
RESEARCH, LLC,**
Respondent.

**ORDER INSTITUTING ADMINISTRATIVE
AND CEASE-AND-DESIST PROCEEDINGS,
PURSUANT TO SECTION 21C OF THE
SECURITIES EXCHANGE ACT OF 1934
AND SECTION 203(e) OF THE
INVESTMENT ADVISERS ACT OF 1940,
MAKING FINDINGS, AND IMPOSING
REMEDIAL SANCTIONS AND A
CEASE-AND-DESIST ORDER**

I.

The Securities and Exchange Commission ("Commission") deems it appropriate and in the public interest that public administrative and cease-and-desist proceedings be, and hereby are, instituted pursuant to Section 21C of the Securities Exchange Act of 1934 ("Exchange Act") and Section 203(e) of the Investment Advisers Act of 1940 ("Advisers Act"), against Athena Capital Research, LLC ("Athena" or "Respondent").

II.

....

III.

....

Summary

1. Athena, an algorithmic, high-frequency trading firm based in New York City, used complex computer programs to carry out a familiar, manipulative scheme: marking the closing price of publicly-traded securities. Through a sophisticated algorithm, Athena manipulated the closing prices of thousands of NASDAQ-listed stocks over a six-month period.

2. Between at least June through December 2009 (the "Relevant Period"), Athena made large purchases or sales of the stocks in the last two seconds before NASDAQ's 4:00 p.m. close in order to drive the stocks' closing prices slightly higher or lower. The manipulated closing prices allowed Athena to reap more reliable profits from its otherwise risky strategies. Internally, Athena called the algorithms that traded in the last few seconds "Gravy."

3. By using high-powered computers, complex algorithms, and rapid-fire trades, Athena manipulated the closing prices of tens of thousands of stocks during the final seconds of almost every trading day during the Relevant Period.

4. Although Athena was a relatively small firm, it dominated the market for these stocks in the last few seconds. Its trades made up over 70% of the total NASDAQ trading volume of the affected stocks in the seconds before the close of almost every trading day.

5. Athena's manipulative trading focused on trading in order imbalances in securities at the close of the trading day. Imbalances for the close of trading occur when there are insufficient on-close orders to match buy and sell orders, *i.e.*, when there are more on-close orders to buy shares than to sell shares (or *vice versa*), for any given stock.

6. Every day at the close of trading, NASDAQ runs a closing auction to fill all on-close orders at the best price, one that is not too distant from the price of the stock in the continuous book. Leading up to the close, NASDAQ begins releasing information, called Net Order Imbalance Indicator ("Imbalance Message"), concerning the closing auction to help facilitate filling all on-close orders at the best price. At 3:50:00 p.m., NASDAQ issues its first Imbalance Message.

7. Athena's general strategy for trading based on Imbalance Messages worked as follows: Immediately after the first Imbalance Message, Athena would issue an Imbalance Only on Close order to fill the imbalance. These orders are only filled if there is an imbalance in a security at the close. Athena would then purchase

or sell securities on the continuous book on the opposite side of its on-close order, until 3:59:59.99, with the goal of holding no positions (being "flat") by the close. It called this process "accumulation," and the algorithms that accumulated these positions were called "accumulators."

8. Athena was acutely aware of the price impact of some its strategies, particularly its last second trading Gravy strategies. Athena used these strategies and its configurations to give its accumulation an extra push, to help generate profits.

9. For example, in April 2009, an Athena manager ("Manager 1"), after analyzing trading in which Gravy accumulated only approximately 25% of its accumulation, and, thus, had no price impact on the stock, e-mailed another Athena manager ("Manager 2") and Athena's Chief Technology Officer ("CTO") suggesting that they: "**make sure we always do our gravy with enough size**" (emphasis added). In fact, Athena traded nearly 60% of its accumulation in the final 2 seconds of the trading day.

10. With the helping hand of its Gravy strategy, Athena refined a method to manipulate the daily process, known as the "Closing Cross," that NASDAQ uses to set the closing price of stocks listed on the exchange. Manipulating the closing process can increase market volatility (thereby frustrating the very purpose of the closing auction) and throw off critical metrics linked to the closing price of stocks. A stock's closing price is the data point most closely scrutinized by investors, securities analysts, and the financial media, and is used to value, and assess management fees on mutual funds, hedge funds, and individual investor portfolios.

11. Athena, however, did not want to push the price of the stocks it traded too much because it created certain trading risks, but also because Athena was concerned about scrutiny from regulators as result of its last second trading. NASDAQ issued an automated Regulatory Alert for "Scrutiny on Expiration and Rebalance Days," which provided that "Suspicious orders or quotes that are potentially intended to manipulate the opening or closing price will be

reported immediately to FINRA." Athena's CTO forwarded this alert to Manager 1 and Manager 2 and wrote: "**Let's make sure we don't kill the golden goose**" (emphasis added).

Respondent

····

Background

13. In late 2003, two former colleagues from a large high-frequency trading firm formed Athena as an algorithmic, high-frequency trading firm.

14. In 2007, Athena sought someone with practical trading experience to help enhance its strategies and develop new ones. In late 2007, Athena hired the Manager 2, as a portfolio manager. Manager 2 introduced Athena to strategies that he and others at Athena referred to as the "Mach" strategies.

15. Athena's Mach strategies focused on trading in securities that were likely to have order imbalances—that is, more orders to buy than sell or vice versa—at the 4:00 p.m. market close.

NASDAQ's Closing Auction and Imbalances

16. During at least the Relevant Period, NASDAQ traders could place several types of orders, known as "on-close" orders, that were only filled at the market close. These order types are not published by any exchange and traders do not know if their orders will be filled until the close.

They included:

a. Limit-On-Close Orders, orders to buy or sell a stock within a specific price range when the market closed;

b. Market-On-Close Orders, orders to buy or sell a stock at the closing price, regardless of what the price was, when the market closed; and

c. Imbalance-Only-On-Close Orders ("Imbalance-Only Orders"), limit orders that would be executed when the market closed, but only if there was an imbalance at the close.

17. Every day at approximately 4:00:00 p.m., NASDAQ ran a closing auction, known as the "closing cross." NASDAQ's proprietary auction algorithm generally set the closing price of each stock to match as many buyers and sellers on the close as possible at a price nearest the last trade on the continuous book, the trades before the close, to reduce volatility.

18. Based on the existing on-close orders for a particular stock, including limit-on-close orders, a closing imbalance of buy or sell orders could occur or disappear as the stock price fluctuated. Leading up to the close, NASDAQ calculated whether, at the then-existing market price for each security, such a closing imbalance would occur.

19. To improve liquidity by encouraging market participants to help fill potential imbalances, NASDAQ informed market participants about the size and direction of predicted closing imbalances during the ten minutes before the close. At 3:50:00 p.m., NASDAQ released a message called a Net Order Imbalance Indicator ("Imbalance Message"). The Imbalance Message contained information for each ticker for which NASDAQ predicted an imbalance based on the then-market price of that stock. The Imbalance Message included the imbalance direction (buy or sell), the size (number of shares predicted to be unfilled at the close), and certain price ranges that could help sophisticated participants estimate the likelihood of an imbalance at a certain closing price. NASDAQ then updated the Imbalance Message, based on the changing market prices and changing on-close orders, every five seconds until the last message at 3:59:55 p.m.

The Mechanics of Athena's Trading Strategy

20. Traders often try to profit from trading on imbalances by taking advantage of expected price increases or decreases when there is more demand for buying a stock than for selling a stock, or vice versa. For example, when an Imbalance Message shows a buy imbalance for a particular stock, meaning there are orders to buy

more shares at the close than orders to sell shares at the close, traders often expect that the stock's closing price will rise to reflect the excess buyer demand. Conversely, when there is a sell imbalance, meaning there are orders to sell more shares at the close than orders to buy shares at the close, traders often expect a lower closing price.

21. Athena's early trading on Imbalance Messages was fairly simple. For example, if the Imbalance Message showed a buy imbalance of 10,000 shares in a particular stock, Athena placed a sell Imbalance-Only Order for 10,000 shares and then tried to accumulate those 10,000 during the next ten minutes before the close. If the Imbalance Message showed a sell imbalance of 10,000 shares, Athena placed a buy Imbalance-Only Order for 10,000 shares and then tried to accumulate a short position of 10,000 shares over the next ten minutes. Athena would exit its position by its on-close order, which, due to the on-close imbalance, was expected to be filled at a better price than the average price at which it accumulated shares.

22. Over time, Athena developed sophisticated strategies for the timing and quantity of its accumulation. Athena's accumulation pattern often involved placing a large order right after the first Imbalance Message, to capture the expected price move due to the published imbalance, then accumulating small amounts of stock over the next nine minutes, followed by a large burst of orders in the final seconds and milliseconds of trading.

23. Athena referred to its accumulation immediately after the first Imbalance Message as "Meat," and to its last second trading strategies as "Gravy." In early 2009, Manager 2 described this pattern in an internal Athena e-mail as follows: "**We have a desired accumulation pattern which includes grabbing stock at the beginning, a period of 'average price' accumulation, and a crescendo at the end**" (emphasis added).

24. During the Relevant Period, Athena used a version of Gravy that placed limit orders in six phases during the last two seconds. For

example, Gravy placed the first order at 3:59:58.35 p.m., the
second at 3:59:58.50 p.m., and so on until the sixth order at
3:59:59.95 p.m., just milliseconds before the close.

25. If a competing order filled the imbalance, Athena was left
with large positions of shares that it had accumulated between
3:50 p.m. through 3:59:59.999 p.m. In other words, if Athena
was not flat at the end of the day, it would incur overnight risk,
and the price of the stock would often move in an unfavorable
direction, resulting in losses, sometimes significant. Athena
referred to this as being "stuck" with those positions.

26. This was particularly problematic for the Gravy strategy—as
Manager 2 pointed out in an e-mail to Manager 1 and the CTO:
**"We can have some aggressive gravy if we know we have a
100% chan[c]e of getting the fill"** (emphasis added).

27. Accordingly, Athena took measures to gain priority over competing limit-on-close orders and Imbalance-Only Orders. As Athena
knew, not all closing trade orders are necessarily executed during
the Closing Cross, and trade orders placed earlier in time are
given priority in the Closing Cross over orders placed later in
time. Similarly, better priced orders are given priority over inferior
priced orders.

28. Athena, therefore, performed sophisticated quantitative analyses,
which it used to place Imbalance-Only Orders prior to 3:50 p.m.
It called this strategy, "Collars."

29. By way of illustration, Athena's trading in shares of EBAY stock
on November 25, 2009, occurred as follows:

- Prior to **3:50 p.m.,** Athena began entering its Collars
  orders.
- **3:50:00 p.m.**—NASDAQ issued its first Imbalance
  Message, which included a 224,638 Buy Imbalance for
  shares of EBAY. At the time, shares of EBAY were trading
  at $23.55.

- **3:50:00.578**—Athena placed a Sell Imbalance-Only Order for 224,638 shares at $.01, and simultaneously placed a buy order of 85,300 shares at $23.56 to begin its accumulation. 16,000 shares were filled almost instantly.
- Between **3:50:07.004** and **3:59:58.112**—Athena placed over 140 limit orders to buy between 100 and 5800 shares of EBAY, purchasing an additional 64,000 shares.
- Milliseconds before 3:59:58, the National Best Offer for EBAY was $23.58, at which point, *Gravy* kicked in, consisting of the following buy orders:

Time	Order Price	Quantity	Exchange
15:59:58.355	$23.81	11,200	BATS
15:59:58.503	$23.81	22,400	BATS
15:59:59.403	$23.81	33,600	BATS
15:59:59.705	$23.81	5,600	NASDAQ
15:59:59.870	$23.81	28,000	BATS
15:59:59.950	$23.81	11,200	NASDAQ

- During this time, Athena bought 112,000 shares (for an average price of $23.594) which constituted over 71% of the entire market volume for EBAY stock in the final two seconds of trading, overwhelming available liquidity and driving up its price.
- **3:59:58.510**—the National Best Offer moved up to $23.59, and at 3:59:59.963, it was $23.60.
- **4:00:03.348**—NASDAQ ran its Closing Cross auction. Athena's Sell Imbalance-Only Orders were filled by selling 233,979 shares for $23.61, $.03 or 13 bps, higher than the best offer in the milliseconds prior to Gravy.

30. As a result of these steps, during the Relevant Period, Athena's Imbalance-Only Orders were filled at least partially over 98% of the time and the firm traded on the entire imbalance of almost

every imbalance it wanted. Athena referred to this in internal e-mails as **dominating the auction** and **owning the game** (emphasis added).

* * *

IV.

In view of the foregoing, the Commission deems it appropriate, and for the protection of investors to impose the sanctions agreed to in Respondent's Offer.

Accordingly, pursuant to Section 21C of the Exchange Act of 1934 and Section 203(e) of the Advisers Act, it is hereby ORDERED that:

A. Respondent Athena cease and desist from committing or causing any violations and any future violations of Section 10(b) of the Exchange Act and Rule 10b-5 thereunder.
B. Respondent Athena is censured.
C. Respondent shall, within 10 days of the entry of this Order, pay a civil money penalty in the amount of $1,000,000 to the Securities and Exchange Commission. If timely payment is not made, additional interest shall accrue pursuant to 31 U.S.C. § 3717. Payment must be made in one of the following ways: ....

By the Commission.

Brent J. Fields
Secretary

We stress that the structured data revealed the pattern; that the pattern justified the subpoenas; and that the e-mails demonstrated the intent to rig the market. The Order interlaces all of this. However, according to a knowledgeable source, finding the pattern in the transactions (the structured data) was not the hard part. It was the e-mails (the unstructured text messages) that were difficult to analyze.

CHAPTER 24

To Know or Not to Know

With all of this going for a litigation early warning system, how could it fail to be a game-changer? We've had more than one person suggest this question: "Wouldn't the attorneys, or the executives, prefer *not* to know?" Or this variation on that theme: "What if the enterprise knew and didn't do anything? If the failure to act, after having knowledge, were to be discovered, wouldn't that be worse than not knowing about the threat in the first place?"

So we must be clear-eyed about this. Our view, to revisit an earlier point, is this:

> [T]he profession needs to rethink its role from that of an ambulance at the *bottom* of a cliff (remedial practice) to helping people to manage risks on *top* of the cliff. While the practice at the bottom of the cliff can be very profitable, clients and consumers should be reminded to avoid practices that are detrimental in the longer run.
>
> To practise [sic] preventive law, we must first work with relevant data. Some of our colleagues may not consider this part of the job description of the legal function, but it is down to us to embrace it or watch someone else do so in the course of taking our profession to the next level. In today's Big Data era, this is not an option, but a *necessity*.[1]

But do attorneys perceive *any* need to change? Historically, the answer is no. As the Hon. John Facciola (U.S. Magistrate Judge, retired) has recounted, "the telephone was in existence for 10 years before lawyers started to use it. They thought it was beneath their dignity."[2]

So, there are obstacles, and we can list some of them. First, we face the momentum in the legal profession that argues against change, especially when the change involves technology. While some of the lawyers who are litigators must now learn to understand technology in the eDiscovery aspects of every lawsuit, they still resist it. Yet many litigators do not know how to use that necessary but admittedly specialized technology.

In fact, they are not even proficient with the basics: software programs for word processing, spreadsheets, and PDFs. And this is why D. Casey Flaherty, formerly in-house counsel at Kia Motors America, and Suffolk University's School of Law recently launched the Suffolk/Flaherty Legal Tech Audit.[3]

In July of 2013, Flaherty explained:

> My hypothesis is that lawyers in general are woefully deficient in using the software tools at their disposal—for example, Word, Acrobat, Excel. To test this, I provided associates at outside firms with mock assignments. Sample tasks include (a) formatting a motion in Word, (b) preparing motion exhibits in PDF, and (c) creating an arbitration exhibit index in Excel.
> I've administered the audit 10 times to nine firms (one firm took it twice). … [A]ll the firms failed—some more spectacularly than others. The audit takes me 30 minutes. So, somewhat arbitrarily, I selected 1 hour as passing. The best pace of any associate was 2.5 hours. Both the median and mean (average) pace rounded to 5 hours.[4]

Second, we face the momentum that has in-house counsel acting as procurement and matter managers of the cases in which an enterprise is involved. They depend on the *bench* of outside law firms to do the heavy lifting.

Third, in-house counsel may balk at having a tool that permits them to take on the mantles of investigator and analyst. Is this the practice of law? Can't the IT or HR departments do this work instead of us?

Fourth, in-house counsel may resist a change that permits them to be strategic business partners with the company's other leaders. Who's in charge?

Fifth, the larger *plaintiff-oriented* law firms may resist any change that reduces the number of prospective plaintiffs. Their reason for being is to redress harm and to recover damages. With fewer deaths, injuries, and other civil wrongs, there would be fewer prospective plaintiffs, and the attorneys who typically only represent plaintiffs would have fewer clients to represent. However, these attorneys can hardly complain if their stated goal is actually achieved, but in some other way. Who can wish for more deaths, injuries, and other civil wrongs?

Sixth, the larger *defense-oriented* law firms may resist any change that reduces the number of lawsuits for them to defend. Their firm revenues are based, in part, on the number of cases they are engaged to defend, and the amount of hours they bill to defend them. They have no financial interest in seeing these metrics go down.

And, any early warning system, at least in its early versions, may produce too many false positives, such that early adopters may look for an early exit and return to their comfort zones. Finally, it could turn out that many business leaders might genuinely prefer to simply deal with lawsuits as they come, to be strictly customer-facing, and to stick with driving revenue.

It seems that there are many reasons *not to know*.

But we contend that we humans have learned, in other contexts, that it is far better to know than not to know. The Greeks knew this long ago, and we have already mentioned their phrase for it: *Forewarned is forearmed*. The ostrich defense—sticking one's head in the sand to avoid knowing about the nearby predator—has never worked very well for the ostrich. In American jurisprudence, this defense is not well known as a successful strategy and has been alternatively called the dumb CEO defense, dummy defense, idiot defense, or Sergeant Schultz defense.[5]

In our view, it is better to suffer through some number of false positives than to be blind-sided by a preventable litigation catastrophe.

We think Bill Gates would agree. In 1999, he wrote a book[6] to which he devoted a whole section and six chapters to explain why. Chapter 10 was entitled, "Bad News Must Travel Fast" He even went a step further, and began the section this way:

I have a natural instinct for hunting down grim news. If it's out there, I want to know about it. The people who work for me have figured this out. Sometimes I get an e-mail that begins, "in keeping with the dictum that *bad news should travel faster than good news*, here's a gem....[7]

Gates provides lots of examples, including from the computer industry. He mentions IBM, when its mainframe and minicomputer businesses were undermined by the PC; Digital Equipment Corporation, when its minicomputer business was undercut by still smaller PCs, which DEC had dismissed as toys; and Wang, which lost the word processing market when it stuck with putting word processing software on dedicated hardware systems rather than on the PC.[8]

He also mentions Ford, Douglas Aircraft, and why the United States was not prepared for the attack on Pearl Harbor.[9]

Gates advised this:

> A change in corporate attitude, encouraging and listening to bad news, has to come from the top.... The bearer of bad tidings should be rewarded, not punished.... You can't turn off the alarm and go back to sleep. Not if you want your company to survive....[10]

Gates asserts that leaders should heed the early warnings from salespeople, product developers, and customers, *but he doesn't mention the Legal Department*. We can excuse the Legal Departments of the past. They had no way to see litigation in-the-making, and so could not sound off to give what Gates called an *alert*.

But now they can. The blinders are off. The revolution is on.

CHAPTER 25

Our Corollary to *Don't Be Evil*

We wrote this book to explain the journey we have taken (so far) to find our way through too much information.

We end this part of our journey by harkening back to Malcolm Gladwell's observation. We have seen that when Big Data meets law and litigation, the problem is not a puzzle where the clues are too few. In the legal space, we have a mystery with too much data, too much knowledge, and *not enough wisdom*.

So here's our answer to that part of the challenge. Google asserts that there is wisdom in its core value: *Don't be evil.*[1] Our corollary is this:

Prevent as much evil as you possibly can.

Notes

Chapter 1

1. For more, go to www.iginitiative.com
2. Blair (2014; italics added).
3. Big Data is not unlike the gargantuan amount of matter that is too small for our eyes to see. To see Big Data, we need technology. For example, a nanometer is one billionth of a meter. Yet the dimensions of DNA (radius, width, and length) are on the order of 1 to 3 nanometers, far too small for humans to see with their own eyes. But when Rosalind Franklin and Raymond Gosling used x-ray diffraction to produce *Photo 51*, James Watson and Francis Crick were able to suggest the first correct *double helix* structure of DNA. See http://en.wikipedia.org/wiki/DNA#History_of_DNA_research. For examples and comparisons, see http://www.nano.gov/nanotech-101/what/nano-size (last accessed on April 7, 2015).
4. Davenport (2015).

Chapter 2

1. Association of Corporate Counsel (2015a).
2. Association of Corporate Counsel (2015b).
3. Association of Corporate Counsel (2015b).
4. Philpin (2013).
5. Philpin (2013).
6. Nick Brestoff's eDiscovery articles are listed on his LinkedIn.com page. In "Can Artificial Intelligence Ease the EDD Burden?," Nick predicted (correctly) that IBM's Watson would prevail in the upcoming *Jeopardy!* competition with two best human champions.
7. With well over 20 years of experience with taxonomies, WAND is the world's leading provider of them. See www.wandinc.com.
8. On June 28, 2013, the authors filed a patent application entitled, "System and Method for Identifying Potential Legal Liability and Providing Early Warning in an Enterprise." U.S. Pat. App. 20130297519. Subsequently, the phrase *early warning* has been used in several other articles: (1) Christopher S. Beach and William R. Schiefelbein's "Unstructured Data: How To Implement An Early Warning System For Hidden Risks" (2014) *Journal of*

Accountancy, www.journalofaccountancy.com/Issues/2014/Jan/20126972. htm (last accessed April 8, 2015), (2) Bennett B. Borden and Jason R. Baron's "Finding the Signal in the Noise: Information Governance, Analytics, and the Future of Legal Practice" (2014) 20 Rich. J. L. & Tech. 7, Vol. 20 pages 29–30, http://jolt.richmond.edu/v20i2/article7.pdf (last accessed on April 7, 2015), and (3) Ralph Losey's "PreSuit"—Detect and Prevent Law Suits Before They Are Filed" (2014), http://e-discoveryteam.com/presuit (last accessed April 14, 2015) (quoting "Finding the Signal").

9. The Latin version of this aphorism (*temet nosce*) was used as an inscription over Oracle's door in the *The Matrix* (1999) and *The Matrix Revolutions* (2003). See http://en.wikipedia.org/wiki/Know_thyself.

10. Brestoff (2012).

11. In 2011, consultant Ron Friedmann espoused bringing the cost of litigation down by doing less of it. See Friedmann (2015). Kenneth Tung urged lawyers to change from remediating damage to clients at the bottom of the cliff in favor of warning them at the top (Tung 2015). ("[T] the profession needs to rethink its role from that of an ambulance at the bottom of a cliff (remedial practice) to helping people to manage risks on top of the cliff.") ("A Kodak moment"). However, in 2008, law practice thought leader Richard Susskind said as much in his book. *The End of Lawyers? Rethinking the Nature of Legal Services* (2008), page 224.

12. Key words often miss their intended target. Consider a traffic accident. The badly injured plaintiff might describe it in terms of *tragedy*, while the drunk driver might think in terms of *accident*. If the plaintiff's attorney asks for all e-mails and other electronically stored information in which the driver described the *tragedy*, the response might be that there are no documents. In a computer, *tragedy* and *accident* are different strings of ones and zeros.

13. Barton (2009).

14. See http://jimgroton.com

15. Barclift (2008).

16. Brown and Brown (1976).

Chapter 3

1. See www.pacer.gov

2. The typical exception arises when a lawsuit is first filed in state court, and then is *removed* to federal court by counsel for one or more of the defendants.

3. In Figure 3.1, the initials SBA stand for the Hon. Saundra Brown Armstrong, Senior District Judge in the Oakland Court house. Initials at the end of a case number refer to the judge assigned to the case.

4. On the PACER Case Locator page, under Nature of Suit, PACER calls NOS code 442 by this variation: Civil Rights: Jobs. We assume that the descriptions are equivalent.

5. We hasten to note that accessing a page in PACER usually costs $0.10, except that there are no additional charges after the first 30 pages. In other words, the maximum per document charge is $3.00. However, there is no charge for court orders.

6. The "well-known conglomerations of tort cases in [multidistrict litigation (MDL)] proceedings include cases concerning breast implants, Baycol, hormone replacement drugs, diet drugs, Seroquel, the September 11, 2001 terrorist attack, Vioxx, Chinese drywall, Deepwater Horizon oil drilling rig, contraceptives, joint implants, and pelvic repair.... [T]he annual number of new cases filed and subjected to MDL proceedings grew from 531 in 1986 to 22,319 in 2012" (Moore 2015, 1213–14).

7. EEOC (2015).

8. Professor Moore considers NOS codes and describes "numerous opportunities for inaccuracy here" (2015, 1208).

9. U.S. Bureau of Labor Statistics (2015).

10. "[T]he only method that does not double-count cases is to measure original filings plus removals from state court. By that measure, civil filings have grown a mere 9 percent since 1986" (Moore 2015, 1181).

11. Moore (2015, 1180).

12. There are far fewer cases filed in MDL category than the number of cases filed in the Civil category and the trend line is not stable, but is instead up-and-down. According to the data in PACER, we report the following: In 2004, there were 24,740 MDL cases filed. In 2005, the number declined to 20,710. In 2006, the number declined again to 15,681. In 2007, the number increased, but only slightly, to 17,724. In 2008, the number nearly doubled to 31,417. In 2009, the number increased again, and substantially, to 45,285. In 2010, the number decreased, but only slightly, to 43,546. Then in 2011, the number of MDL cases dropped to only about 40 percent of the previous year to 17,278. In 2012, the number recovered, but only slightly, to 25,043. But in 2013, the number reached an all-time high, at 52,615. Thus, during the same period from 2004 to 2013, there were 295,039 MDL cases filed, which is only a little over 10 percent of the 2,827,193 civil cases. While the average size of MDL settlements and verdicts may be substantially higher than they are in commercial torts in the Civil category, we have no data to support any conclusions.

13. If we add the number of Cases Filed in PACER in 2014 (303,357), the total crosses the 3 million mark, to 3,130,550 for the 11-year period from 2004. This addition increases the average number of Cases *Filed* per year to 284,595. By comparison, the total number of Cases *Closed* during the same 11-year period was 2,977,550, an average per year of 270,686.

14. Though *habeas corpus* cases are Civil cases, and there were years in which there were more than 10,000 such cases filed, we do not show them because they are not business-relevant.

15. We do not mean to suggest that Asbestos is a flash-in-the-pan matter. It has been called the longest-running mass tort in U.S. history. (See http://en.wikipedia.org/wiki/Asbestos_and_the_law.) It bankrupted the Manville Corporation (formerly the Johns-Manville Corporation) in 1980s when it ranked 181st on the Fortune 500 list, and bankrupted more than a dozen other companies during the 1990s.

16. In 2014, according to PACER, the number of NOS code 368 (Asbestos) cases filed against Fluor was back down to only 17.

Chapter 4

1. Mayer-Schonberger and Cukier (2013) call a combination of datasets *recombinant* data.

2. See www.ncsc.org.

3. See www.lexmachina.com.

4. Lex Machina (2014). Note: Lex Machina reported attorneys' fees when they were awarded, but not otherwise. Thus, the median compensatory award does not include them. In the 2014 Patent Litigation Year in Review, Lex Machina reported a compensatory damages median of approximately $420,000 for all damages awarded in cases filed since the year 2000.

5. The mean and median are the same only in the case of a perfect bell-curve shaped distribution.

6. Schuchman (2015).

Chapter 5

1. *United States v. Lauren Stevens* (2011; emphasis added).

Chapter 6

1. With thanks to Norman Thomas, Senior VP Corporate Development of Litera, we could have constructed a different Litigation 100 out of the larger set, namely the Fortune 500.

2. Fortune.com (2015).

3. Per PACER, the number of Civil cases filed between 01/01/2012 and 12/31/2012 was 277,856.

4. Fortune.com (2013).

5. U.S. Chamber of Commerce Institute for Legal Reform (2012).
6. Since the federal court caseload was 1,248,327, the ratio is about 2.18 to 1.

Chapter 7

1. We are skipping two steps. The first step is to open PACER.gov. The second step is to login. Anyone can log in once they set up an account. PACER is open to the public, not just attorneys.
2. Our calculations understate Xerox's total litigation cost and the cost as a percentage of Net Profits because the data reflects *only* the federal court data, and does not include data from the 50 states. We cannot say how the marketplace for Xerox's stock would be affected by this incomplete data, if at all.
3. For our more tech-savvy readers, select the Download button, and choose the right hand option (CSV). PACER will download the caseload data responsive to your search criteria and do so in spreadsheet format. The spreadsheet can be cleaned up in a way that will suit the reader and then it can be recorded as an Excel spreadsheet.

Chapter 8

1. Brown (1950).
2. Drucker (1963).
3. See Chapter III – Strategic Attack ("It is best to win without fighting.") in *The Art of War* (6th century BC), https://en.wikiquote.org/wiki/Sun_Tzu.
4. See www.ushistory.org/franklin/quotable/quote67.htm.
5. See http://en.wikipedia.org/wiki/Praemonitus_praemunitus.
6. Davis (2008).

Chapter 9

1. *Spandow v. Oracle America, Inc.* (2014; italics added).
2. *Sharma v. Atlas Aerospace, LLC* (2014; italics added).
3. *Cogburn v. Montgomery County Nursing Home Board* (2014; italics added).

Chapter 10

1. For a more technical and complete discussion of the differences between repetitive and nonrepetitive data, see W. H. Inmon and Dan Linstedt's *Data Architecture: A Primer for the Data Scientist: Big Data, Data Warehouse and Data Vault* (Elsevier Morgan Kaufman, 2014).

2. Bill's software is not NLP based and does not use NLP approaches to deal with context. In the "She's hot" example, he argues that, while NLP attempts to understand the context of words by looking at other words, context is much more than words. See http://forestrimtech.com/textual-etl/ textual-etl-technology. However, for a series of recent videos describing *deep learning* text analysis, including NLP, we direct our readers to the presentations at Text By the Bay 2015, held on April 24–25, 2015, and published on or above June 10, 2015 by YouTube.com.

3. See http://en.wikipedia.org/wiki/That_that_is_is_that_that_is_not_is_not_ is_that_it_it_is.

4. We cite quite a few *Wikipedia* references in this book. We do so with the understanding that, in the past, *Wikipedia* has been criticized as being unreliable. However, we believe that *Wikipedia* is far less unreliable than in the past, and we note that we have not written this book to pass muster in an academic setting.

5. See http://en.wikipedia.org/wiki/Ford_(disambiguation).

6. Bill explained in a recent video (published March 5, 2015) that it is the visualization of *context* from deeply unstructured text that matters to decision makers. See Visualizing Unstructured Data with Tableau, Featuring Bill Inmon, at www.youtube.com/watch?v=tDtkyMfT-F8, (accessed May 4, 2015). The video is just over 39 minutes long.

7. See http://en.wikipedia.org/wiki/War_and_Peace (sidebar: length of the first published edition), (accessed May 4, 2015).

Chapter 12

1. Taxonomies are used as filters when the data is scanned to obtain the output.

Chapter 13

1. The visualization video in endnote 5 of Chapter 11 pertains to data from a call center.

Chapter 14

1. Hadoop is an open source framework for distributed storage and processing of very large data sets on clusters of computers. See http://en.wikipedia.org/ wiki/Apache_Hadoop (last accessed on May 4, 2015).

2. See www.wandinc.com

Chapter 15

1. StatisticBrain.com (2014).
2. Credit: J. Greim/Science Source.

Chapter 16

1. Grush and Saunby (1973); Ivey (1973).
2. http://en.wikibooks.org/wiki/Professionalism/The_Ford_Pinto_Gas_Tank_Controversy (accessed on May 4, 2015).
3. Dowie (1977).
4. See http://en.wikipedia.org/wiki/Ford_Pinto.
5. Gary T. Schwartz's "The Myth of the Ford Pinto Case" 43 Rutgers L. Rev. (1990–1991), pages 1013, 1017. The Schwartz article pertains to the case of *Grimshaw v. Ford Motor Co.*, 119 Cal. App. 3d 757, 174 Cal. Rptr. 348 (1981). In that case, which went to trial in 1978, a California jury awarded wrongful death damages of $560,000, $2,500,000 in compensatory damages, and punitive damages of $125 million. However, the trial court reduced the punitive damages award to $3.5 million. The appellate court upheld that ruling and the California Supreme Court subsequently denied further review. While the jury's punitive damages award may seem *over the top*, it should be noted that the trial judge had *not* permitted the Ford Pinto Memo to be admitted into evidence. Had the judge done so, the initial verdict could have been even larger, which indicates that members of a jury can be harsh when the jury has evidence that a business values profits over lives, serious injuries, and safety.
6. *Arthur Andersen LLP v. United States*, 544 U.S. 696 (2005) (jury verdict reversed due to erroneous instructions on the law to the jury). For the story of the Enron debacle and the e-mail cited in the text, see Kurt Eichenwald's *Conspiracy of Fools: A True Story* (New York: Broadway Books, 2005), page 529. More generally, see Mimi Swartz and Sherron Watkins's *Power Failure: the Inside Story of the Collapse of Enron* (New York: Doubleday, 2003).
7. See *Salisbury v. City of Pittsburgh* (2010).
8. International Litigation Services (2013).
9. Bruce (2011).
10. See Laura Zubulake's historic fight to discover the e-mails recovered from backup tapes and other sources, and how a few of those e-mails played a significant role in the trial against her former employer (2012, 17–34).

Chapter 18

1. To support in-house counsel, however, some portion of the IT department needs to be dedicated to the prevention effort.
2. We thank University of Colorado Law Professor Harry Surden for making this point. See Surden (2014). The investment figures are from Clark (2015).
3. *Wultz v. Bank of China* (2013) (emphasis added—quoting *In re Grand Jury Subpoena*, 599 F.2d 504, 511 (2d Cir. 1979)).
4. *Wultz v. Bank of China* (2013, 487) (internal citations omitted).
5. *Wultz v. Bank of China* (2013, 488) (emphasis added).
6. See *Upjohn Co. v. United States* (1981) (adopting a version of the subject matter test). In *Upjohn*, the Supreme Court said that "the privilege exists to protect not only the giving of professional advice to those who can act on it but also the giving of information to the lawyer to enable him to give sound and informed advice." In that case, the attorney-client privilege protected interview notes and memos by in-house counsel conducting an internal investigation into illegal payments by employees. Furthermore, the primary purpose test does not require showing that obtaining or providing legal advice was the *sole* purpose of an internal investigation or that the communications at issue would not have been made *but for* the fact that legal advice was sought. See *In re Kellogg Brown & Root, Inc.,* 756 F.3d 754 (D.C. Cir. 2014). For another recent case, holding that an attorney memorandum regarding her advice during a contract negotiation was legal advice (for which the attorney-client privilege applied), and was *not* business advice (for which the privilege did *not* apply), see *Exxon Mobil Corp. v. Hill (EMC),* 751 F.3d 379 (5th Cir. 2014). Note that the codification of the attorney-client privilege is not uniform throughout the country, and readers should consult their own counsel.
7. *Faragher v. City of Boca Raton* (1998) (emphasis added).
8. EEOC (2000).
9. EEOC (2000).
10. *EEOC v. Fred Meyer Stores, Inc.* (2013).

Chapter 19

1. 191 Cal.App.4th 1047, 119 Cal.Rptr.3d 878 (2011).
2. See 17 Misc. 934, 847 N.Y.S.2d 436 (2007).
3. *In re Asia Global Crossing, Ltd.*, 322 B.R.247 (S.D.N.Y.) (2005).
4. *Quon v. Arch Wireless Operating Co.*, 529 F.3d 892 (9th Cir. 2008), *rev'd on other grounds by City of Ontario, Cal. v. Quon*, ___ U.S. ___, 130 S.Ct. 2619, 177 L.Ed.2d 216 (2010) (reversing on Fourth Amendment grounds

only); see also *City of Ontario*, 130 S.Ct. at 2627 ("The petition for certiorari filed by Arch Wireless challenging the Ninth Circuit's ruling that Arch Wireless violated the SCA was denied.").

5. *Stengart v. Loving Care Agency, Inc.* (2010).
6. *Mintz v. Mark Bartelstein & Assoc., Inc.* (2012).
7. *Mintz v. Mark Bartelstein & Assoc., Inc.* (2012).
8. Olson (2014).
9. See 15 U.S.C. 45(n). The FTC can enforce this prohibition using administrative remedies or judicial remedies, or both, including in a federal court proceeding in which civil penalties or injunctions may be sought (15 U.S.C. 45(b) and 53(b)). The FTC argues that the scope of its authority is broad because Congress intentionally did not define *unfair* and left it to the FTC to do so. *See* the FTC's Brief in *Federal Trade Commission v. Wyndham Hotels & Resorts, LLC*, No. 14-3514 at pp. 16-17 (3rd Cir. Nov. 14, 2014). www.ftc.gov/system/files/documents/cases/141105wyndham_3cir_ftcbrief.pdf (last accessed April 8, 2015).
10. The broadness of the FTC's authority is being challenged in an interlocutory appeal to the Third Circuit. See *Federal Trade Commission v. Wyndham Hotels and Resorts, LLC*, Case No. 14-3514 (3d Cir. 2014).

Chapter 20

1. EDRM.net (2014).
2. Doherty (2014).
3. EDRM.net (2015).
4. Here is an example of a *power* key word search using Boolean connectors: "(successor/5 corporation) /p (toxic or hazardous or chemical or dangers/5 waste) /p clean! And (aft 1/1/90)." In plain language, this search is for cases where a successor corporation is liable for the cleanup of hazardous waste after January 1, 1990.
5. Blair and Maron (1985).
6. Tomlinson et al. (2008). "Overview of the 2007 TREC Legal Track." The references to TREC in this and the following endnote are to the Legal Track of the Text Retrieval Conference (TREC), which is administered by the U.S. National Institute of Standards and Technology.
7. Oard et al. (2009).
8. Landauer and Dumais (1977).
9. Brestoff (2010).
10. See http://en.wikipedia.org/wiki/Taxonomy_(general) ("Many taxonomies have a hierarchical structure, but this is not a requirement.")
11. Hedden (2010, 119, 123–25).

Chapter 21

1. NHTSA (2014, 5).
2. NHTSA (2014, 6).
3. NHTSA (2014, 8).
4. GM recalled 2.6 million vehicles worldwide because the ignition switch defect "causes the switch to slip into the accessory position, shutting down the engine and disabling electrical systems—including air bags" Bronstad (2015, 13).
5. Bronstad (2015, 8).
6. Bronstad (2015, 11).
7. See Associated Press, http://abcnews.go.com/Business/wireStory/gm-ignition-switch-death-toll-switches-rises-97-30788318 (last accessed May 4, 2015).
8. Gara (2014).
9. Gara (2014). Gara's blog attracted several comments. One was "So I can't use "Corvair-like?" Pinto it is." Another wrote: "At Ford, we used to be encouraged to say "Thermal Event" instead of fire. That stopped around 2005, when the attorneys told us to explain things with normal words. Basically, they told us to use our heads and say what happened. The Firestone fiasco really drove a safety culture into Ford, one that GM is just learning." Courtney Love wrote, "Kurt would be so happy about this!" Gara's blog article included the NHTSA Consent Order.
10. Shakespeare's *The Tempest* (*circa* 1610), Act 2, Scene 1.
11. For background facts, see *Grimshaw v. Ford Motor Co.* (1981).
12. Gooden (2009, 26–34).
13. See Chapter 11, footnote 2.

Chapter 22

1. NOS code 445 pertains to Civil Rights: Americans with Disabilities—Employment. We don't know why this particular tort was separated out from NOS code 442, but we note that it would make sense for PACER to assign NOS codes to the other EEOC categories.
2. Taylor (2015).

Chapter 24

1. "A Kodak moment," see endnote 11 in Chapter 2.
2. Facciola (2015).

3. Flaherty and Perlman (2015). ("The test takers will finalize a redlined investors' rights agreement (word processing). They will then be given data on dividend payments to investors to investigate whether payments were made equally to all investors (spreadsheets). Finally, they will prepare an e-filing attaching the agreement and spreadsheet (PDF).")
4. Flaherty (2013).
5. U.S. Legal, Inc. (2015).
6. Gates and Hemingway (1999, 159–200).
7. Gates and Hemingway (1999, 159–60).
8. Gates and Hemingway (1999, 179–80).
9. Gates and Hemingway (1999, 180). For the Pearl Harbor example, Gates cites Gordon Prange's *At Dawn We Slept* (New York: McGraw Hill, 1981) at 439–92 (Chapters 54 through 59), for communications breakdowns and "fundamental disbelief" on the U.S. side during the weekend of December 6–7, 1941.
10. Gates and Hemingway (1999, 179).

Chapter 25

1. Levy (2011, 144–46).

References

Association of Corporate Counsel. 2015a. "About ACC: The World's Largest Community of In-House Counsel." http://www.acc.com/aboutacc/index.cfm (accessed April 7, 2015).

Association of Corporate Counsel. 2015b. "ACC Value Challenge." www.acc.com/valuechallenge (accessed April 7, 2015).

Barclift, Z.J. 2008. "Preventive Law: A Strategy for Internal Corporate Lawyers to Advise Managers of Their Ethical Obligations." *Journal of the Legal Profession* 33, p. 31.

Barton, T.D. 2009. *Preventive Law and Problem Solving: Lawyering for the Future*. Lake Mary, FL: Vandeplas Publishing.

Blair, B.T. 2014. "Is the Biggest Risk of Big Data the Inability to Extract Value?" Information Governance Initiative. http://iginitiative.com/biggest-risk-big-data-inability-extract-value/ (accessed April 12, 2015).

Blair, D.C., and M.E. Maron. 1985. "An Evaluation of Retrieval Effectiveness for a Full-Text Document-Retrieval System." *Communications of the ACM* 28, no. 3, pp. 289–99.

Borden, B.B., and J.R. Baron. 2014. "Finding the Signal in the Noise: Information Governance, Analytics, and the Future of Legal Practice." *20 Richmond Journal of Law & Technology* 7. http://jolt.richmond.edu/v20i2/article7.pdf (accessed April 7, 2015).

Brestoff, N. Autumn 2010. "E-Discovery Search: The Truth, the Statistical Truth, and Nothing but the Statistical Truth." *American Bar Association's E-Discovery and Digital Evidence Journal* 1, no. 4, pp. 2–20.

Brestoff, N. 2011. "Can Artificial Intelligence Ease the EDD Burden?" *Legaltech News*. www.legaltechnews.com/id=1202478529697/Can-Artificial-Intelligence-Ease-the-EDD-Burden?slreturn=20150528140353 (accessed June 28, 2015).

Brestoff, N. 2012. "Data Lawyers and Preventive Law." *Legaltech News*. www.legaltechnews.com/id=1202576202439/Data-Lawyers-and-Preventive-Law?slreturn=20150308102523 (accessed April 8, 2015).

Bronstad, A. May 2015. "Prepping Their Best—Litigators Are Getting Ready to Try Bellwether GM Ignition Switch Cases." Corporate Counsel. http://www.corpcounsel.com/id=1202723243820/Prepping-Their-Best.

Brown, L.M. 1950. "Manual of Preventive Law." *New York: Prentice Hall, Inc.*

Brown, L.M., and H.A. Brown. 1976. "What Counsels the Counselor? The Code of Professional Responsibility's Ethical Considerations—A Preventive Law Analysis." *Valparaiso University Law Review* 10, no. 3, pp. 453–77.

Bruce, S. September 2011. "The $6.9 Billion Smoking Gun E-mail." HR Daily Advisor—BLR.com. http://hrdailyadvisor.blr.com/2011/09/20/the-6-9-billion-smoking-gun-e-mail/ (accessed April 8, 2015).

Clark, J. February 2015. "I'll Be Back: The Return of Artificial Intelligence." *Bloomberg Business.* www.bloomberg.com/news/articles/2015-02-03/i-ll-be-back-the-return-of-artificial-intelligence (accessed July 19, 2015).

Cogburn v. Montgomery County Nursing Home Board, Case No. 6:14-cv-06024-SOH (W.D. Ark. 02-21-2014).

Davenport, T.H. 2015. "Let's Automate All the Lawyers." *The Wall Street Journal.* http://blogs.wsj.com/cio/2015/03/25/lets-automate-all-the-lawyers/ (accessed on April 7, 2015).

Davis, D.S. 2008. "Right Turn at the Right Time." UPS Pressroom. http://pressroom.ups.com/About+UPS/UPS+Leadership/Speeches/D.+Scott+Davis/Right+Turn+at+the+Right+Time (accessed April 8, 2015).

Doherty, S. October, 2014. "Myth Busting Predictive Coding: Are Key Words Really Dead?" *Legaltech News.* www.legaltechnews.com/id=1202674375517/MythBusting-Predictive-Coding-Are-Key-Words-Really-Dead?slreturn=20150314113937 (accessed April 14, 2015).

Dowie, M. September/October 1977. "Pinto Madness." Mother Jones. www.motherjones.com/politics/1977/09/pinto-madness?page=1 (accessed April 8, 2015).

Drucker, P. May 1963. "Managing for Business Effectiveness." *Harvard Business Review*, p. 83.

EDRM.net. 2014. "New EDRM Diagram Emphasizes Information Governance." http://www.edrm.net/archives/23174 (accessed April 11, 2015).

EDRM.net. 2015. "Computer Assisted Review Reference Model (CARRM)." www.edrm.net/resources/carrm (accessed April 11, 2015).

EEOC v. Fred Meyer Stores, Inc., Case No. 3:11-cv-00832-HA at 4 (D. OR September 19, 2013).

Facciola, J. April, 2015. "Law at the Speed of Technology: Q&A with John Facciola." By Zoe Tillman. Corporate Counsel, p. 56.

Faragher v. City of Boca Raton, 524 U.S. 775, 806-807 (1998).

Flaherty, D.C. July 2013. "Could You Pass This In-house Counsel's Tech Test? If the Answer Is No, You May Be Losing Business." ABA Journal. www.abajournal.com/legalrebels/article/could_you_pass_this_in-house_counsels_tech_test (accessed April 8, 2015).

Flaherty, D.C., and A. Perlman. 2015. Suffolk/Flaherty Legal Tech Audit. www.legaltechaudit.com (accessed April 8, 2015).

Fortune.com. 2013. "Fortune 500 2013: See Our Methodology." http://fortune.com/fortune500/2013/ (accessed April 20, 2015).

Fortune.com. 2015. "Fortune 500 2014." http://fortune.com/fortune500/ (accessed April 8, 2015).

Friedmann, R. 2015. "Do Less Law 2014 Recap: Value Via Prevention and Doing Less." Prism Legal. http://prismlegal.com/?s=February+10%2C+2014 (accessed April 8, 2015).

Gara, T. May 2014. "The 69 Words You Can't Use at GM." *The Wall Street Journal.* http://blogs.wsj.com/corporate-intelligence/2014/05/16/the-69-words-you-cant-use-at-gm/ (last accessed April 8, 2015).

Gates, W.H.B., III, and C. Hemingway. 1999. *Business @ the Speed of Thought: Using a Digital Nervous System.* New York: Warner Books, Inc.

Gooden, R.L. 2009. *Lawsuit! Reducing the Risk of Product Liability for Manufacturers.* Hoboken, NJ: John Wiley & Son, Inc.

Grimshaw v. Ford Motor Co., 119 Cal.App.3d 757 (1981).

Grush, E.S. and C.S. Saunby. 1973. "Fatalities Associated with Crash Induced Fuel Leakage and Fires." The Center for Auto Safety. www.autosafety.org/uploads/phpq3mJ7F_FordMemo.pdf (accessed April 8, 2015).

Hedden, H. 2010. *The Accidental Taxonomist.* Medford, NJ: Information Today, Inc.

International Litigation Services. January 2013. "E-mail Threads and Chains as Evidence: The Smoking Gun of Plaintiff eDiscovery." Plaintiff eDiscovery and eDiscovery Database Experts. www.ilsteam.com/email-threads-and-chains-as-evidence-the-smoking-gun-of-plaintiff-ediscovery (accessed April 8, 2015).

Ivey, E. 1973. "Value Analysis of Auto Fuel Fed Fire Related Fatalities." CNN. www.cnn.com/US/9909/10/ivey.memo (1999 transcript) (accessed April 8, 2015).

Landauer, T.K. and S.T. Dumais. 1977. "Solution to Plato's Problem: The Latent Semantic Analysis Theory of Acquisition, Induction and Representation of Knowledge." *Psychological Review* 104, no. 2, pp. 211–40.

Levy, S. 2011. *In the Plex—How Google Thinks, Works, and Shapes Our Lives.* New York: Simon & Schuster.

Lex Machina. 2014. Lex Machina Patent Litigation Damages Reference Sheet. https://lexmachina.com/wp-content/uploads/2014/12/Damages-Reference-Sheet.pdf (accessed April 8, 2014).

Mayer-Schonberger, V., and Cukier, K. 2013. *Big Data: A Revolution That Will Transform How We Live, Work, and Think*, 107. New York: Houghton Mifflin Harcourt.

Mintz v. Mark Bartelstein & Assoc., Inc., 885 F.Supp.2d 987, 998 (C.D. Cal. 2012).

Moore, P.W.H. 2015. "The Civil Caseload of the Federal District Courts." *University of Illinois Law Review* 1177. http://papers.ssrn.com/sol3/papers. cfm?abstract_id=2416864 (accessed on June 8, 2015).

NHTSA (U.S. National Highway Traffic Safety Administration). May 2014. Consent Order in NHTSA's Timeliness Query, In re TQ14-001, NHTSA Recall No. 14V-047.

Oard, D.W., B. Hedin, S. Tomlinson, and J.R. Baron. March 2009. "Overview of the 2008 TREC Legal Track." http://www.ece.umd.edu/~oard/pdf/trecov08.pdf

Olson, P. November, 2014. "Fitbit Data Now Being Used in the Courtroom." Forbes. www.forbes.com/sites/parmyolson/2014/11/16/fitbit-data-court-room-personal-injury-claim (accessed April 16, 2015).

Philpin, A. 2013. "8 Vendors in Gartner's 'Magic Quadrant for Enterprise Legal Management." http://zonese7en.com/8-vendors-in-gartners-magic-quadrant-for-enterprise-legal-management/ (accessed April 7, 2015).

Salisbury v. City of Pittsburgh, Case No. 08-cv-0125 (W.D.Pa. 2010).

Schuchman, L. May 5, 2015. "Trademark Litigation Report Finds $9B in Damages." Corporate Counsel. http://www.corpcounsel.com/id=1202725 526110/Trademark-Litigation-Report-Finds-369B-in-Damages#ixzz 3ZIUMe8Os (accessed May 5, 2015).

Sharma v. Atlas Aerospace, LLC, Case No. 6:14-cv-01057-CM-KMH (D.C. Kan. 02-22-2014).

Spandow v. Oracle America, Inc, Case No. 3:14-cv-00095-EDL (N.D. Cal. 01-07-2014).

StatisticBrain.com. 2014. "Corrective Lens Use Statistics." www.statisticbrain. com/corrective-lenses-statistics (accessed April 11, 2015).

Stengart v. Loving Care Agency, Inc., 990 A.2d 650 (N.J. 2010).

Surden, H. 2014. "Machine Learning and Law." University of Washington Law Review 87. http://digital.law.washington.edu/dspace-law/bitstream/ handle/1773.1/1321/89WLR0087 (accessed July 2, 2015).

Taylor, C.K. 2015. "How to Calculate the Margin of Error: What Is the Margin of Error for an Opinion Poll?" Statistics—About.com. http://statistics.about. com/od/Inferential-Statistics/a/How-To-Calculate-The-Margin-Of-Error. htm (accessed April 8, 2015).

Tomlinson, S., D.W. Oard, J.R. Baron, and P. Thompson. April 2008. "Overview of the 2007 TREC Legal Track." http://trec.nist.gov/pubs/trec16/papers/ LEGAL.OVERVIEW16.pdf

Tung, K. March 24, 2015. "A Kodak Moment for the Legal Profession." Lexology. www.lexology.com/library/detail.aspx?g=2eae2fe3-8226-45b2-931e-97b7d66ed7d1 (accessed April 11, 2015).

U.S. Bureau of Labor Statistics. 2015. "Consumer Price Index—All Urban Consumers (2004-2013)." http://data.bls.gov/pdq/SurveyOutputServlet (accessed April 8, 2015).

U.S. Chamber of Commerce Institute for Legal Reform. 2012. 2012 State Liability Systems Survey—LAWSUIT CLIMATE—Ranking the States. www.instituteforlegalreform.com/uploads/sites/1/Lawsuit_Climate_Report_2012.pdf (accessed April 8, 2015).

EEOC (U.S. Equal Opportunity Employment Commission). July 2000. "Enforcement Guidance: Compensatory and Punitive Damages Available Under Section 102 of the Civil Rights Act of 1991, Section II.A (1)." www.eeoc.gov/policy/docs/damages.html (accessed April 8, 2015).

EEOC. 2015. "Discrimination by Type." http://www.eeoc.gov/laws/types/index.cfm (accessed April 8, 2015).

U.S. Legal, Inc. 2015. "Ostrich Defense Law and Legal Definition." http://definitions.uslegal.com/o/ostrich-defense/ (accessed April 27, 2015).

United States of America v. Lauren Stevens, Case No. 8:10-cr-00694-RWT (03-23-2011).

Upjohn Co. v. United States, 449 U.S. 383 (1981).

Wultz v. Bank of China, 979 F.Supp.2d 479 (S.D.N.Y. 2013).

Zubulake, L.A. 2012. *Zubulake's e-Discovery: The Untold Story of My Quest for Justice.* New York: Laura A. Zubulake.

Index

OTHER TITLES IN OUR BUSINESS LAW COLLECTION

John Wood, Econautics Sustainability Institute, Editor

FORTHCOMING TITLES FOR THIS COLLECTION

- *Light on Peacemaking: Mindful Mediation of Family Conflict* by Thomas DiGrazia
- *Consumer Bankruptcy: A Guide for Businesses* by Scott B. Kuperberg

Business Expert Press has over 30 collection in business subjects such as finance, marketing strategy, sustainability, public relations, economics, accounting, corporate communications, and many others. For more information about all our collections, please visit www.businessexpertpress.com/collections.

Business Expert Press is actively seeking collection editors as well as authors. For more information about becoming an BEP author or collection editor, please visit http://www.businessexpertpress.com/author

Announcing the Business Expert Press Digital Library

Concise e-books business students need for classroom and research

This book can also be purchased in an e-book collection by your library as

- a one-time purchase,
- that is owned forever,
- allows for simultaneous readers,
- has no restrictions on printing, and
- can be downloaded as PDFs from within the library community.

Our digital library collections are a great solution to beat the rising cost of textbooks. E-books can be loaded into their course management systems or onto student's e-book readers.
The **Business Expert Press** digital libraries are very affordable, with no obligation to buy in future years. For more information, please visit **www.businessexpertpress.com/librarians**. To set up a trial in the United States, please email **sales@businessexpertpress.com**.

Printed in the USA
CPSIA information can be obtained
at www.ICGtesting.com
LVHW020337181223
766747LV00011B/778